THE *Art* OF CONFIDENT Living

10 PRACTICES FOR TAKING CHARGE OF YOUR LIFE

Bryan Robinson, Ph.D.

Health Communications, Inc.
Deerfield Beach, Florida

www.hcibooks.com

**Library of Congress Cataloging-in-Publication Data
is available through the Library of Congress.**

© 2009 Bryan E. Robinson, Ph.D.
ISBN-13: 978-07573-0651-8
ISBN-10: 0-7573-0651-9

HCI, its logos, and marks are trademarks of Health Communications, Inc.

Publisher: Health Communications, Inc.
          3201 S.W. 15th Street
          Deerfield Beach, FL 33442-8190

Cover design by Justin Rotkowitz
Interior design and formatting by Dawn Von Strolley Grove

❧ Contents ❧

iii

❧ Acknowledgments ❧

I want to acknowledge the people whose support made it possible for me to complete this project.

I want to thank my agent, Sally McMillan, for her tireless efforts in promoting my work and Sara Thompson, Linda Hamilton, Dr. Julie Maccarin, Kevin Davis, Dr. Pat Love, and Chris Burris for their feedback on early versions of this manuscript. A special thanks goes to Maggi Saucier, who read the manuscript meticulously and offered invaluable recommendations.

To my partner, Jamey McCullers, I am deeply appreciative for his enduring love and support, which had my back as I pounded away at my computer.

I am especially indebted to Dr. Richard Schwartz, whose Internal Family Systems model has had a profound impact on my personal and professional life. I appreciate his generosity with his ideas, some of which are woven throughout this revised edition, and his constructive feedback on early versions of the manuscript.

And my deepest love and appreciation to the Caring Presence that I'm getting to know with greater clarity and connectedness with each passing day.

❧ Introduction ❧

We believe that everything there is to find is out there in the light where it's easy to find, when the only answers for you are in you!

—Leo Buscaglia

The dead aren't supposed to walk among the living, but they do. I know they do, because I was one of them. Many years ago, emotionally dead, I slumped in my airplane seat. When the flight attendant asked me if I wanted something to eat, all I could do was wave her away with my hand. I had lost so much weight that I looked like a refugee from Dachau, the Nazi concentration camp. During liftoff, I didn't care if the plane crashed. Nothing mattered. I was on my way for a sunny week in Jamaica to escape the pain of the breakup of a fourteen-year relationship.

My life was crumbling under my feet, and there was nothing I could do. I didn't care if I lived or died. I was already dead inside, an empty shell from defining myself by my outside life—relationship, career, and material things. Once they were gone, so was I, or so I thought.

Legions of emotionally dead people walk among us, focused on finding the right mate, getting promoted, making more money, and buying that vacation home. These are all great things to have, but they mean nothing without a strong connection to yourself. Things are temporary. They rust, erode, decay, and die. Material gain—a new house, car, or money—can bring temporary highs that flatten out after only a short while. Regardless of whether life throws us highs or lows, it is our internal life that keeps us steady in a sea of ups and downs and carries us over the long haul.

When material things are gone, so are we—unless we have an inner life to undergird them. When we do, things can vanish and our strength is sustained. That is what this book is about—finding the *Confident Self* within and living from the inside out instead of from the outside in.

ROADBLOCKS TO
THE CONFIDENT LIFE

Here's a checklist of roadblocks to the Confident Life. Do any of them apply to you?

❑ Do you beat yourself up for what you "should" have done?

❑ Do you put up resistance to keep things as they are?

❑ Do you react to life, rather than take action when problems or worries befall you?

❑ Do you believe you are a victim of life circumstances?

❑ Do you hold on to resentments?

❑ Do you find yourself expecting the worst or worrying about bad things happening?"

❑ Do you let fear dominate your life?

❑ Do you think more about "what if" instead of "what is"?

❑ Do you feel unworthy?

❑ Are you a perpetual people pleaser?

❑ Do you neglect yourself in favor of others?

❑ Do you look for things outside yourself to make you happy?

❑ Have you used geographic escape to run from your problems?

About This Book

This book can help you develop a solid, strong inner world that brings out the confidence that exists naturally within you, and it can help you navigate through whatever life brings.

It has been almost twenty years since the first version of this book, *Heal Your Self-Esteem*, hit bookstores. Since that time, we have entered into a new century, and much has happened in our culture that is relevant for a book of this nature. When this book first appeared, the Internet, laptops, BlackBerrys, iPods, PDAs, Wi-Fi, and e-mail did not exist. Now the workday phrase "9 to 5" has become obsolete, replaced by the new millennium phrase "24/7." Not that long ago, speed dating and online matchmaking didn't exist, and we had not experienced the events that shattered our sense of national security on 9/11 and prompted the official "War on Terror." Since 1991, our country has undergone a cultural revolution in terms of foreign affairs, technology, workplace issues, family dynamics, and relationships—all factors impacting our confidence levels.

This revised edition is a makeover of the earlier book to reflect these cultural changes. The 10 Principles, which I developed for the previous edition, recast in this edition as the 10 Practices, remain the backbone of the book. This edition has been updated with groundbreaking research on confidence, some of which was nonexistent when the previous edition was written. Much of the new research has closed the divide between the findings of scientists and mystics. More and more, the research has substantiated the 10 Practices, many of which have been around for centuries.

In writing this book, I have drawn on my personal experiences, the research I've conducted for the past twenty years, my vast clinical experience, and findings from top experts from around the world. This revised edition, written in a readable way, contains lots of new examples and stories that have been updated for the twenty-first century. It combines scientific knowledge, clinical case studies, personal accounts, and simple techniques—all the ingredients necessary for you to lead a confident life.

The Art of Confident Living is a practical guide for connecting with the confidence inside you and achieving joy and serenity every day. The 10 Practices give you techniques that put you in harmony with yourself and free you from your past. They show you how to achieve a full and satisfying life in the present by assembling all the ingredients you need *now* to be confident, regardless of what or why certain events happened in the past. These 10 Practices, when applied in your daily life, will bring out the confidence you've been seeking and improve the quality of your life.

The 10 Practices can help you to achieve the following:

• Get that dream job you always wanted
• Find the soul mate you've been seeking

- Boost your immune system and physical health
- Achieve the goals you've set in life
- Reduce job stress and burnout
- Eliminate bad habits and addictive behaviors
- Improve your performance in any sport you play
- Promote a healthier and happier lifestyle and increase longevity
- Feel more comfortable and have more fun in social situations
- Be admired by others
- Minimize worry and face life's challenges as adventures to have instead of problems to solve
- Have more energy and joy in your life

In writing this book, I realize that I have written a thousand different books. You will read the words on the page differently because of what you already think and believe. You will filter the words through your perceptual systems and will select and use what you need in order to profit from your individual life journey. As you become more confident from the inside out, confidence will love you back from the outside in.

Chapter One

The 10 Practices

Taking Charge of Your Life

Don't look outside yourself for the leader.
—*Hopi Indian saying*

Living From the Inside Out

Everyone wants to live a confident, fulfilling life. So why are so many people miserable so much of the time, constantly searching with little success? The reason is that we get caught up in our outside lives and lose track of who we are on the inside. If confidence or lack of it is created on the inside, doesn't it make sense that to find it you would start there?

Twenty-two-year-old Amy worked for a computer company in New York City. She was bored and weary of the morning grind: rush hours, fast-paced routines, and traffic jams. She had few friends and was generally unhappy with her life. Finally, with her mother's encouragement, Amy decided to move to California to "find herself." After a few months, she decided that Los Angeles "was not what it was cracked up to be," so she moved to Seattle, where she finally faced the truth: her unhappiness was inside of her, and that was where she needed to focus.

Unfortunately, geographic escape doesn't help us find ourselves. Our inner selves are not waiting on some faraway street corner for our bodies to catch up. We simply pack up old habits and carry them like luggage wherever we go. The surroundings are different, but our responses are the same. If we wake up feeling positive and optimistic in Detroit, we wake up feeling positive and optimistic in the Mediterranean. If we wake up to anxiety and pessimism in Buffalo, we wake up to anxiety and pessimism in the South Pacific. The grass is not greener in another place.

Those of us who feel incomplete and empty often look outside ourselves to correct bad habits or fill an inner void. Take Mario, a physician who didn't feel he'd earned the right to live unless he was working. Hospitalized for depression, Mario had been putting in seventy-hour workweeks and was still behind. His need for approval was insatiable, and nothing seemed to satisfy his craving for accolades, power, and importance. Even the workaholism that he'd turned to swallowed him up and hadn't been enough to fight off the depression that eventually won the battle.

Lynn is another case in point. She once told me, "My confidence is defined by what I can produce, and that provides my identity. I associate whether I have worth and value with what I achieve, and if I am not achieving, then I have no worth or value. It's like who I am depends on whether I'm able to achieve, not that I'm a good person, not that I have a lot of good qualities. But if I achieve, I have worth and value. That's real distorted, but that's where I'm at."

Like Mario and Lynn, many of us seek confidence through accolades, overloading ourselves with projects, deadlines, and busy activities. Or we use alcohol, unhealthy relationships, food, and possessions to build confidence. We become enslaved by greed, competition, power, wealth, and material gain, thinking they are answers to our problems. We search frantically for purpose through jobs, relationships, drugs, cars, or big homes. We expect our careers, kids, love interests, Dr. Phil, or Oprah to give us the answers. We rearrange our furniture, change jobs, divorce and remarry, establish new friendships, buy a new wardrobe, change our hair color, build a new house, have children—all in an effort to lead a Confident Life.

The Israeli leader Golda Meir once observed, "At work,

you think of the children you have left at home. At home, you think of the work you've left unfinished. Such a struggle is unleashed within you. Your heart is rent." Nevertheless, rearranging the exterior circumstances of our lives doesn't provide what we seek when it's an inside job that's needed.

The Dalai Lama contrasted two life situations to show how happiness is determined more by state of mind than external events.[1] The first was a woman who prospered from a financial windfall as a result of a profitable business investment. Her meteoric success suddenly gave her lots of money, free time, and retirement at a young age. After the dust settled from her newfound wealth, her life returned to normal, and the woman said she was no happier than before the windfall.

Contrast her situation to a second one in which a man of about the same age contracted HIV. Devastated at the news, the young man spent a year getting over the shock and disbelief. However, by taking the opportunity to explore spirituality for the first time, he found his life transformed in positive ways. He seemed to appreciate everyday things more and to get more out of each day than ever before, and he felt happier than he had before the diagnosis.

Scientists and spiritual leaders agree on few things, but they do agree that material things don't buy confidence. The studies on happiness, for example, show that wealth, marital status, age, beauty, and other external variables do not make people any happier or more confident—even though most people think they will. Physically attractive people aren't happier, and people with disabilities aren't more miserable. Happiness and confidence are not by-products of life circumstances. They are by-products of our state of mind—the ways in which we experience our lot in life.

Material gain—a new house, a new car, or more money—can bring us temporary highs that usually flatten out after a short time. Tragedy or loss can put us at an all-time low for a while, but eventually our moods rise back to normal. Regardless of highs and lows, most of us keep going back to a baseline of happiness. So, if we keep returning to a certain baseline regardless of our life conditions, what determines our level of happiness? The answer is internal conditions, which keep us steady in a sea of ups and downs and carry us for the long haul. When misfortune hit, the man afflicted with HIV refused to become a victim, turning his obstacle into an opportunity to become an *active* participant in life rather than a *passive* recipient of what life doled out.

Living Out Loud

Many of us live below life's radar instead of living out loud, and because we don't see the water we're swimming in, we don't realize we could be sabotaging our confidence. I spent much of my life believing that I was a victim of my dysfunctional family upbringing. This illusion put bars on a cage, which imprisoned me—without me knowing it—with the belief that I had no say over my life. That mental prison restricted me to living in quiet desperation below life's radar, instead of living freely and fully. As a young adult, the cycle of misery continued just as if my alcoholic father (who had died five years earlier) were still in control of my fate.

As I began to liberate myself through the 10 Practices, I no longer saw myself as a disempowered victim of circumstances. By freeing myself from the illusion, I learned to live from inside out, to make free choices, and to see that I could take responsibility for my life conditions. With the mind-set of a survivor, instead of a victim, I surrendered to situations over which I had no control, and I moved out of my life what I did not want and made room for what I did want. My whole life changed inside out and outside in as a result of these 10 Practices (see page 7 for a list of the 10 Practices).

Sam, who lived four years with lung cancer, decided that, regardless of how many days he had left, he'd live as large as possible, and that's exactly what he did. He didn't hold anything back. He fully embraced his feelings, hugging whomever he felt like hugging, forging bonds with people unlike any he had ever forged before. He adopted his own dress code, expressed his opinions freely, spoke out on important issues, and stood his ground even when it went against the grain. The people around him admired this uncharacteristic side of him.

THE 10 PRACTICES

You can lead a Confident Life with the 10 Practices:

1. *The Practice of Separation:* Practice separating your Confident Self from your ego parts.
2. *The Practice of Perception:* Practice freeing yourself from negative illusions of the past that eclipse who you really are.
3. *The Practice of Choice:* Practice remembering that you have choices, from moment to moment, no matter how difficult the situation.
4. *The Practice of Optimism:* Practice looking for the positive, instead of the negative, even in the most challenging situations.
5. *The Practice of Empowerment:* Practice thinking of yourself as a survivor, instead of a victim, and accepting responsibility for your lot.
6. *The Practice of Harmony:* Practice surrendering to conditions over which you have no control and making the best of them.
7. *The Practice of the Unmade Mind:* Practice keeping your mind unmade, instead of made up, in new situations.
8. *The Practice of Vacuum:* Practice moving out of your life what you *don't* want to make room for what you *do* want.
9. *The Practice of Magnetism:* Practice attracting people and situations into your life that mirror the confident images you hold of yourself.
10. *The Practice of the Boomerang:* Practice projecting confidence from within that will come back into your life in one form or another.

The best people from whom to learn how to live with confidence are those facing past or present seismic events. When seismic events (e.g., childhood trauma, terminal illness, death of loved ones, and loss of a job) bulldoze through our lives, life is no longer an academic exercise. It wakes us up to the fact that we can no longer afford to let our circumstances define us. It shakes our foundation into change so that we begin to create a life from the inside out. However, the good news is that we do not have to wait for a crisis to create a Confident Life. We can have it now without urgency. We get no guarantees about tomorrow, but we can live a Confident Life today.

The 10 Practices put you on the riverbank of your life so that you can see the water you are swimming in—clarity to see your life through new eyes and objective tools to change it for the better. Or, as Teilhard de Chardin put it, "ever more perfect eyes in a world in which there is always more to see."

The 10 Practices help you acknowledge your strengths and weaknesses, ask for help or admit you're wrong without feeling shame or ineptness, and stand up for your opinions instead of seeking approval. They free you from self-doubt and strengthen belief in yourself—belief that you can make things happen and get things done. They free you from the internal prison you've created with negative illusions that eclipse your Confident Self, helping you live large with your priorities rearranged from the inside out.

When you live a Confident Life, you move out of your life what you *don't* want so that you can create positive life conditions that you feel responsible for instead of victimized by. You project confidence through thoughts, feelings, and actions that come back to enrich your life in one form or another and to attract people and situations that reflect your inner confidence. The 10 Practices build upon one another in a stepwise fashion, and you don't have to go find them because you already have them inside of you.

Scientific Underpinnings of the 10 Practices

None of us with a sound mind would leap off a ledge into the Grand Canyon because we know that if we defy the law of gravity, we'd fall down and not up. Yet many of us leap off the cliff of our personal lives every day. When our lives aren't working, we can't understand why. We keep getting involved in unhealthy relationships that hurt us. We go back to the same people for the same rejections. We keep trying to solve problems in the same old ways that we already know don't work. We resist change and cling to sameness. We live in the past or future instead of the present. We set goals that are unrealistic or out of reach, and we neglect and condemn ourselves daily. The list is long. The 10 Practices can help you change those aspects of your life that aren't working.

If someone held an apple and let it go, you would predict

that it would fall to the ground. Your prediction would be based partly on your past experience and on the gravitational pull of Earth. Sir Isaac Newton discovered the law of gravity as he sat under an apple tree. When an apple dropped to the ground near him, he wanted to know why the apple fell down and not up. From this simple incident, Newton developed the law of gravity to explain the behavior of Earth and the planets, moon, sun, stars, and asteroids.

You don't defy the law of gravity because you know you'd be asking for trouble. You avoid touching the metal handles of hot cooking pots without a pot holder because you know a physical principle is operating: metal conducts heat. You also refrain from touching an exposed wire while standing in the bathtub because you know the result could be lethal. The operating principle you're using then is *water conducts electricity.* Because you know these principles to be true, you obey them.

Similar principles govern our thoughts, feelings, actions, the nature of our relationships, and the quality of our lives. Because these principles are not as precise as the laws of physics, we keep making the same mistakes and continue to find ourselves in the same unworkable conditions that result in disillusionment and loss of confidence.

In the last ten years, science has credited many age-old opinions: the brain wants to heal old wounds, meditation and optimism help us live longer, optimists move up the corporate ladder quicker and easier, prayer works, we see what we expect to see, and a view of nature from a hospital window can contribute more to recovery from surgery than medication. Scientists at the National Institutes of Mental Health now report that the brain has the ability to change its wiring and grow new neural connections through regular practice and repetition of tasks. In other words, you have an innate ability to transform your mind by changing old ways into new ones. This, in turn, reshapes your nerve cells and changes the way your brain works. In *The Art of Happiness*, the Dalai Lama and Howard Cutler explain the implications of the brain's ability to change its neural connections:

> It (this ability) is also the basis for the idea that inner transformation begins with learning (new input) and involves the discipline of gradually replacing our "negative conditioning" (corresponding with our present characteristic nerve cell activation patterns) with "positive conditioning" (forming new neural circuits).[2]

What this boils down to is that science says you can become more confident by changing how you use your mind. One of the most effective ways is through meditation, which quiets the mind so that you can hear what is already there. This quieting gives you insight into yourself and restores inner harmony and balance so that you are more harmonious with the world and the people in it. Heart rate and brain wave patterns slow down during meditative states. Going within has a positive effect on the immune system and body chemistry, too, in that certain hormones are secreted that have life-sustaining qualities. Scientists now know that adults who meditate each day actually have fewer health problems and live longer than adults who do not. In other words, the scientific world underscores the value of going within and connecting with the Confident Self that resides inside all of us.

Science also now states that people who lead Confident Lives not only live longer but live happier and tend to have fewer addictive behaviors. They have a clear-mindedness about who they are and a clarity of life purpose. One confident person said that compassion for others was the best high she could ever have. In fact, compassionate givers have brain scans that indicate better emotional health, more calm, less depression, and greater self-worth than takers do. Perhaps science has given a whole new meaning to the old adage "It is better to give than to receive."

In his book *The Tao of Physics*, physicist Fritjof Capra described how the Eastern spiritual disciplines and modern physics converge:

> I was sitting by the ocean one late summer afternoon, watching the waves rolling in and feeling the rhythm of my breathing, when I suddenly became aware of my whole environment as being engaged in a gigantic cosmic dance. Being a physicist, I knew that the sand, rocks, water and air around me were made of vibrating molecules and atoms, and that these con-

sisted of particles which interacted with one another by creat-ing and destroying other particles. I knew also that the earth's atmosphere was continually bombarded by showers of "cosmic rays," particles of high energy under-going multiple collisions as they penetrated the air. All this was familiar to me from my research in high-energy physics, but until that moment I had only experienced it through graphs, diagrams and mathemati-cal theories. As I sat on that beach, my former experiences came to life; I *saw* cascades of energy coming down from outer space, in which particles were created and destroyed in rhyth-mic pulses; I *saw* the atoms of the elements and those of my body participating in this cosmic dance of energy; I felt its rhythm and I *heard* its sound and at that moment I *knew* that this was the Dance of Shiva, the Lord of Dancers worshipped by the Hindus.[3]

In much the same way, the 10 Practices parallel the physi-cal laws. They bring a scientific undergirding to the idea that happy, successful outer lives are created from the inside out from confident internal lives. As you understand and apply these 10 Practices, just as you do the physical laws, you'll see them work (see page 14). As you see them work, you'll feel more confident that you can change your life. That con-fidence strengthens your willingness to let your Confident Self lead your life.

ARE YOU LEADING YOUR LIFE WITH CONFIDENCE?

Are you living out loud or below the radar? Are you a people pleaser? Do you question yourself? Do you waffle or fold under pressure? Are you driven by "should haves," "what ifs," and other self-defeating messages? Do you put others' needs before your own, living your life for everyone but yourself? If so, confidence might be a no-show in your life. To find out, answer yes or no to each of the following questions:

1. Do you seek approval from others through people pleasing?
2. Do you judge yourself harshly?
3. Do you resist change?
4. Would you trade your life for someone else's?
5. Do you spend a lot of time getting upset or angry over things you can't control?
6. Are you afraid to let other people get close to you?
7. Do you waffle or fold under pressure?
8. Do you feel that you're not enough and need someone or something to be complete?
9. Do you usually put your needs behind those of others?
10. Do you question your ability to do things?
11. Do you feel worthy of other people's love?
12. Do you believe you can turn a bad situation into a good one most of the time?
13. Do you look on the bright side instead of the dark side in most situations?
14. Do you enjoy your own company?
15. Are you open to new ideas or different ways of doing things?
16. Do you expect the best out of most situations?

17. Do you believe in yourself?
18. Do you tend to praise yourself or give yourself pep talks?
19. Is it easy for you to express your true feelings?
20. Are you open-minded?

Scoring: Start with 60 points. Subtract 2 points for each *yes* answer to questions 1 to 10. Add 2 points for each *no* answer to questions 1 to 10. Subtract 2 points for each *no* answer to questions 11 to 20. Add 2 points for each *yes* answer to questions 11 to 20.

YOUR CONFIDENCE REPORT CARD:

Scores	Grade	Interpretation
Below 60	F	Low: Your Confident Self is still hibernating, and you're living below the radar.
60–69	D	Below average
70–79	C	Average
80–89	B	Good
90 100	A	Excellent: You're living with your Confident Self leading the way.

Regardless of how high or low you scored, don't despair. The following chapters will give you some tried-and-true confidence-building practices to guide you to a better life all around. As you start to lead your life with *confidence*, you might remain the same person on the outside. You might keep the same job and the same relationships. You still might feel angry or impatient, sad or disappointed, sometimes. Your transformation will happen on the inside. You will look at your life in a different way. You will see with new insight and greater clarity, and you will take different actions that will create a more **Confident Life.**

Chapter Two

The Practice of Separation

Separating your Confident Self from your ego parts

One day, to our astonishment, we will find that the True Self for which we are searching is also searching for us.

—*Stephen Cope*

The Confident Self

Curtis is a physician who felt he had to take on every referral from colleagues—even if he was not sure the patient's problem fell within his area of expertise. His approval-seeking mind-set continued to get him into trouble because he often found himself in medical situations that were over his head. Curtis unwittingly allowed his *approval seeker* (an ego part) to run his life instead of his Confident Self.

If you are a Confident Person, your Confident Self is at the helm, you know who you are on the inside, and you are faithful to yourself. You do what you believe to be right, regardless of other people's opinions. You are a creative risk taker who stretches beyond customary bounds while also knowing your limits. You are a master of self-correction, learning from your mistakes instead of covering them up. You can say no with confidence, instead of shame, if something is beyond your scope of ability. You have a solidness, a sureness about you. You tend to live your life from the inside out, instead of the outside in, with balance, openness, acceptance, and joy.

For many of us, the Confident Self gets eclipsed by parts of our ego, and we tend to identify with our ego parts more than with the Confident Self. Confidence is not something you have to seek outside yourself. It exists naturally within you, but for many of us it has been eclipsed by our ego parts. In the words of the spiritualist Eckhart Tolle, "Outflow determines inflow. Whatever you think the world is withholding from you, you already have, but unless you allow it to flow out, you won't even know that you have it."[1] (See page 19 for more about the eight qualities of the Confident Self, which this book explores in greater depth from chapter to chapter.)

EIGHT QUALITIES OF
THE CONFIDENT SELF

In his book *Introduction to the Internal Family Systems Model,* psychotherapist Richard Schwartz described eight "C" qualities that will help you know when you're in touch with your Confident Self.[2]

In this book I draw upon his eight "C" words to describe the Confident Self:

- A sense of *clarity* and direction
- An unmistakable feeling of infectious *calm*
- A *connectedness* within yourself and with others
- More *curiosity* and less judgment of self and others
- Heightened self-*confidence*
- Increased susceptibility to *compassion* for self and others
- Greater *courage* to face life's challenges
- Bursts of *creativity* that let you think outside the box

These eight qualities, which reflect your true nature, are peppered throughout this book.

When you are in one or more of these states of consciousness, you know that your Confident Self is in the lead. As you read further, you can discover them within yourself and feel your confidence start to shine through.

The Confident Relationship

Jeff couldn't talk to his wife about marital issues. Instead of hearing what he said, she crumbled when he brought up concerns because she heard them as the same criticisms she got from her parents while she was growing up. Jeff said his only recourse was to stuff his feelings, which came out sideways as resentment toward her. He snapped at her or made snide comments, and she couldn't understand why. This is an example of what a Confident Relationship is not.

In his book *The Seven Principles for Making Marriage Work*, John Gottman identified four red flags that indicate a relationship is headed south: criticism, defensiveness, contempt, and withdrawal.[5] These four warning signs typify a relationship that has closed shop. In contrast, the Confident Relationship is open for business—both parties are willing to communicate about problems and concerns. Neither party in a Confident Relationship is interested in conflict, judging, criticism, or in interpreting each others' actions. Instead, they strive for a harmonious connection through empathy and respect for the other's point of view. Overwhelming episodes of appreciation are frequent, and both partners are susceptible to receiving love and have an uncontrollable urge to extend it. Richard Schwartz described the Confident Relationship this way:

Clients' relationships became more harmonious, or they found the courage to leave relationships that had been exploitive. They became less reactive in crises and less overwhelmed by emotional episodes that used to do them in.[4]

The "I" in the Storm

Most of us have a kick-butt voice that lives inside our heads, putting us under the microscope, telling us how inadequate, selfish, or bad we are. Much like the hard-ass drill sergeant who is trying to save his soldiers' lives, the critical mental thought pattern points out our failures and judges our flaws. It often gets more airplay than the inner chitchat that tells us how great we really are. Richard Schwartz calls the inner voice *a part* of ourselves. Buddhists, like nun Pema Chodron, refer to it as *ego,* and spiritual teachers Eckhart Tolle and Anthony de Mello call it *the thinker* or *conditioned mind.* Anthony de Mello sums it up this way:

My upset does not come from outside reality, but from my inner conditioning. Remove the conditioning and the upset disappears. My way of thinking and of looking at things, my principles and judgments, even my tastes and preferences are the result of the long process which has been my living in a particular family, school, church, and societal framework. That framework has shaped my mind, channeled my thoughts, and has determined how I must react "spontaneously" to facts and situations. . . . To recognize that my upsets come from myself is the first step to remedying them.[5]

Spiritualist Marianne Williamson called the ego the *great fault finder.* And Mohandas Gandhi said, "Many could forego having meals, a full wardrobe, a fine house, et cetera; it is the ego they cannot forego." When your ego or ego parts lead your life, they eclipse your "I" or Confident Self. (*EGO* then stands for *Ease God Out.*) These experts all agree that the goal is to separate your Confident Self from the conditioned voice (i.e., part, ego, or conditioned mind) and keep it at arm's length.

Your Ego Is Your Friend

The ego has gotten a bum rap. I've been in meditation circles where we were told to leave our egos outside with our shoes or to somehow burn up the ego or get rid of it. These messages set up an adversarial relationship between my Confident Self and ego parts, creating even more internal frustration and chaos within me. Once I realized this approach was a mistake and that I couldn't get rid of my ego no matter how hard I tried, I changed course. I began to understand how my ego parts were trying to help me and that I needed them as much as my brain or stomach to function in life. This realization brought about a major shift within me — more serenity and comfort inside my own skin. The mind is an organ, designed to protect itself at all costs. Just as the rib cage protects the lungs, we have ego protector parts that protect our psychological vulnerabilities. Sometimes parts don't budge, and they insist on leading our lives. The mind uses these illusions to protect us, especially from things that have harmed us in the past. Like the Energizer Bunny, the ego parts keep on going and going— protecting us in the present the same way they did when we were six or seven years old.

When in the blink of an eye an ego part takes over, it doesn't always feel warm and fuzzy. "How could my judgment or criticism part be my friend when it feels so harsh and unrelenting?" you might ask. To that I say that some parts operate much like the kick-ass drill sergeant who doesn't want us getting our heads blown off in combat. Sometimes parts might feel so unpleasant that your first impulse might be to ignore, get angry with, or try to extinguish them. As you begin to look beneath the surface at a part's intent, though, instead of identifying yourself as the part, you'll see that it is *always* trying to help.

I am reminded of a time when I had a low-grade fever that made me sluggish and my concentration difficult. I had trouble working and took frequent naps. I underwent every test known to humankind, all the results of which were negative. I became frustrated and resentful of my fever because it kept me from being on top of my game, or so I thought. When it finally dawned on me that my fever was protecting me— fighting off foreign agents that could harm me—I changed my course of action. I befriended my fever, sending it love and support, and the next day it was completely gone. In much the same way, it can feel like ego parts are working against us when, in fact, they are working hard to protect us from a threat or to get us what they feel we need for a good life.

In trying to help, ego parts often eclipse your Confident Self because they think they know what's best for you from moment to moment. Once you appreciate the earnest intent of your ego parts and develop a working relationship with them, instead of identifying with them, your Confident Self will shine through.

The 10 Practices can help you be in the world in a way that makes you conscious of your ego parts, reminding you that your Confident Self can take the lead. The first step in this process is to separate from your ego parts so that you can get better acquainted with them—that is the Practice of Separation.

The Practice of Separation

Making the separation from your ego parts can be one of life's greatest achievements. In his widely acclaimed book *A New Earth: Awakening to Your Life Purpose*, Eckhart Tolle described the initial difficulty of the separation process:

> Most people are still completely identified with the incessant stream of mind, of compulsive thinking, most of it repetitive and pointless. There is no 'I' apart from their thought processes and

the emotions that go with them. This is the meaning of being spiritually unconscious. When told that there is a voice in their head that never stops speaking, they say, "What voice?" or angrily deny it, which of course *is* the voice, is the thinker, is the unobserved mind. It could almost be looked upon as an entity that has taken possession of them.[6]

Many of us think of and refer to ourselves in ways that reflect what people have told us over the years. Through conditioning, these messages become *parts* of us. You might call yourself negative, selfish, shy or a control freak, worry wart, sad sack, penny pincher, workaholic, alcoholic, or caretaker. The list is endless. Even if you are what you call yourself, that trait only describes a *part* or aspect of you, not *all* of you—for example, if you're a worry wart, your worry is not you. If it was you, you'd worry 24/7, and no one worries every second of the day. You have a Confident Self apart from your worry, apart from your judgment, apart from your doubt. Still, you have been taught to define yourself by parts of you and to look outside yourself to correct any problems, instead of finding solutions inside.

Within all of us is an "I" or Confident Self that has been eclipsed by the parts of ourselves with which we have identified since we were young. If I think of myself as a control freak, then that identity eclipses the rest of me. If I think of myself as an angry person, then it is difficult for me to know the rest of me. If I think of myself as a selfish person, then I probably won't like myself very much because I'm not able to see my positive qualities. However, if I think of my controlling nature, anger, or selfishness as parts or aspects of who I am, then I've separated from my parts and started to make room for deeper insight into the rest of me.

Richard Schwartz described the *clarity* clients achieve when they successfully make the separation between a part and the Confident Self:

> During such episodes (upsetting situations), they would say the difference was that they knew it was a part of them, that not *all* of them was that upset, so rather than blending with the part, they would notice it and then try to comfort it. They didn't always succeed in calming it down, but just the awareness that they were not the part helped them remain the *"I" in the storm.*[7]

How many times have you had a sinking feeling when you had to make a presentation, stand in front of a group of people, or perform in some other way? If you stop and think about it, you'll notice that the feeling comes from an inner voice (a part of you) that predicts you'll mess up. This voice keeps you from believing in yourself. Otherwise, why would you worry?

Suppose you have your eye on a certain job for which you're qualified or that you're attracted to a person but you don't have the *confidence* to go after the job or the person. That, too, happens because something is in the way of your believing in yourself. You might be holding irrational, unconscious judgments that you're completely unaware of such as *They're bound to dislike me; I've felt like a failure all my life, and I can't bear to fail again;* or *I'll never be good enough for them.* These judgments reverberate in your mental echo chamber from a part of you—a part from which you can separate. After all, no objective evidence exists for any of these beliefs because you haven't even taken the first step to apply for the job or speak to the person you find attractive. Philosopher Marcus Aurelius said, "If you are distressed by an external thing, it is not this thing which disturbs you, but your own judgment about it. And it is in your power to wipe out that judgment now."

Since the time of Aurelius, we've discovered that it's impossible to wipe out the judgment part of ourselves (or any part of the ego for that matter). Nor would you want to, because you need this part, and all your other parts, to function fully. So, even though you can't get rid of the part that judges, you can develop a relationship with it by stepping back and listening to it with *curiosity* as often as you can. In the words of Pema Chodron:

> So whether it's anger or craving or jealousy or fear or depression—whatever it might be—the notion is not to try to get rid of it, but to make friends with it. That means getting to know it completely, with some kind of softness and learning how, once you've experienced it fully, to let it go.[8]

Next time the negative voice blinks in your mind like a neon sign, listen to it as a separate part of you, not all of you. Listening to it as a separate part, instead of as you, gives you distance from it and can help you appreciate that it is actually trying to protect you in its own way. Because it thinks you will fail, its intention might be to stop you in your tracks to keep you from failing so that you won't feel badly about yourself.

Curiosity is the gateway to separation and a Confident Life. Mustering as much curiosity about the part and listening to it impartially—with curiosity instead of judgment—keeps you from attacking yourself. If you refrain from judging, you'll notice an ease in seeing what's there. Ask your judgment part if it can relax so you can be curious. Then, think of the voice as a friend who is trying to help you in his or her own way—a friend whom you'd like to get to know better. You might even imagine the part sitting across the room from you in a chair as you have a conversation with it, or you might let your curiosity write the part a letter. In his book *The Power of Now*, Eckhart Tolle described the separation this way:

Pay particular attention to any repetitive thought patterns, those old gramophone records that have been playing in your head perhaps for many years. . . . When you listen to that voice, listen to it impartially. That is to say, do not judge. Do not judge or condemn what you hear, for doing so would mean that the same voice has come in again through the back door. You'll soon realize: *there* is the voice, and here *I am* listening to it, watching it. This *I am* realization, this sense of your own presence, is not a thought. It arises from beyond the mind.[9]

The Internal Boardroom

Once you employ the Practice of Separation, the clouds part inside and your Confident Self shines through. One way to achieve this separation is to imagine that you have an internal boardroom where all life decisions are made. Let's take my internal boardroom to show you what I mean: I am the CEO of my organization known as Bryan Robinson. I imagine that I sit at the head of a long table in a conference room. In any given situation I have certain parts that show up at that table ready for action. These parts are stockholders in my organization, and each one wants a say in how I, the CEO, run my life.

A random thought or feeling or an upsetting situation can trigger parts to take over my internal organization. One afternoon, for example, I'd just finished seeing clients and had come out of my office. On a desk in the waiting room I saw some papers, a book, and a check that a client had neatly stacked for me. It had been the first session for the bright, corporate executive, suffering from stress and burnout. I had given her a book to read and some forms to complete for the next session. Obviously, she wasn't impressed with my recommendations and wanted to show it by leaving the suggestions I had made, along with payment for the session, as if to say "Thanks, but no thanks!"

All week I wondered what had gone wrong. During dinner, driving to and from work, and out with friends, I'd catch myself replaying the session in my mind and agonizing over how I'd misjudged what I had thought to be a great session. Although we had made another appointment for the next week, I figured she wouldn't show. To my surprise she did show up for her appointment with a sheepish look on her face, and said, "I've dreaded this appointment all week. I'm afraid you're going to think I'm a bad patient. But I have to confess that I misplaced the forms and book you gave me, and I haven't done my homework. I've looked everywhere and can't find them."

I chuckled inside when I realized the self-judgment parts of both of us had overthrown our *CEOs* (Confident Selves), kicking us out of our respective chairs at the head of the table, putting us through needless mental torture, making us miserable. Through the eyes of my judgment part I'd been incompetent, while my client's judgment part told her she was unreliable. Because they came from the judgment part, not from the CEO (Confident Self) or the objective facts of the situation, neither belief was true. Once the judgment part took over my organization, other parts—such as *worry, frustration,* and *another judgment part*—showed up at the conference table, freaking out over my incompetence. There even might have been another part that wanted to drink several glasses of wine to calm down the worry and frustration. My internal boardroom might be in complete chaos for an entire week because my judgment part (which says, *I'm incompetent*) had taken over.

The way to fix this, of course, is for my Confident Self (CEO) to have a relationship with the judgment part at the outset. When I find the client's neatly stacked items, I'd look inside myself with curiosity and imagine me staying seated at the head of the table. As I notice the judgment part jumping to conclusions without evidence, I would ask the judgment to stay in its seat and relax. With the curiosity of a private detective, I might ask the judgment, "Where's the evidence for this conclusion?" In most cases, no hard facts support the judgment's conclusion, because its belief is based on inside feelings, not outside, objective evidence.

The goal in such emotional situations is for my Confident Self (CEO) to have a relationship with each of the parts so that they don't feel they have to take over to save the day. I would acknowledge the other upset parts, seeing if they would be willing to relax, let them know that I understand their upset and that I will handle the situation for them. In other words, instead of the parts taking over and going off the launch pad, I might speak to the parts as if they are individual people. When I practice separating from my parts and suspending conclusions until the hard evidence is in, I develop relationships with my parts that ignite calm inside me and impact how I live my life on the outside.

When we can do this, we create more calm inside ourselves and more harmony with others. Richard Schwartz calls this *Self-Leadership:*

> When they (clients) were in that calm, compassionate state, I asked these clients what voice or part was there. They each gave a variation of the following reply: "That's not a part like those other voices are, that's more of who I really am, that's my Self."[10]

Let's look at another example of this shift. Brad was having trouble concentrating on his golf game and his guitar lessons. Every time he stepped up to tee off, he overthought his strategy. The same thing happened with his guitar lessons, and Brad continued to fail miserably and feel badly about himself. When I asked him to look curiously inside and identify what part or parts were at his internal boardroom table, he said an inner voice was saying *I'm gonna screw up* and another was saying *What are people gonna think of your bad performance?*

I suggested to Brad that he check out the concerns of the voices or parts *before* he performed and to develop an understanding of their motives. He learned that his ego parts were trying to prepare him for the inevitable failure that they expected. Using the Practice of Separation, his Confident Self reassured the parts by saying *I've got this covered*, and by doing this he was able to get them to relax. He shot the best golf game ever, and his guitar playing improved by leaps and bounds.

Performance in many arenas can be enhanced when we give all parts at the table a voice, instead of trying to ignore or stifle them. Once they have had their say and feel heard as a stockholder by you, they are often willing to settle down and let the Confident Self run the show.

Once you are able to hear the voice as a *part* of you instead of as *you*—without wasting energy being frustrated with it or trying to get rid of it—the more room your Confident Self will have to lead with the calm, confident, compassionate voice that cheers you on with good-hearted pep talks and affirmations like a best friend would. You will know you are at the helm when you are in any of the eight "C" states referred to as the Confident Self throughout this book. One of the most significant changes that can ever happen to you is set in motion within as you begin the process of separating your *ego parts* from your *Confident Self*.

Living the Practice of Separation

The parts of ourselves (or our conditioned minds) can be all engulfing to the point that we think they are who we are. Separating from your parts is an inside job. The following practices can help you get some distance from your parts so that you (Confident Self) can lead your life from the inside out instead of the outside in.[11]

What It Feels Like When Confidence Leads Your Life

Recall the feeling you get after recognition for an accomplishment at work, when you buy a new car or move into a new place, when you've won a game, or when you're proven right in an argument. Now contrast those feelings with how it feels when you're bursting with love for another human being, watching a brushed-magenta-colored sunset, wading the surf with waves lapping at your bare feet, holding a newborn close to your breast, feeling compassion for someone you've helped, savoring calm after meditating or praying, or overflowing with confidence before a challenging task.

Notice the qualitative difference between the first set of worldly feelings, which feed the insatiable appetite of the ego, and the second set of feelings, which come from the Confident Self. Notice how you feel in the two different experiences and which is more fulfilling and sustaining. In their attempts to satisfy the ego with worldly pleasures, many people lose their soul in external, empty lives. As you move through week to week, pay attention to how many of your actions are ego driven versus Confidence driven, and ask yourself if you'd like to move in a different direction.

Your Internal Boardroom

One way to practice separation and put confidence in the lead is through the boardroom meditation. Over the years, many of my clients have used this approach and found it to be incredibly beneficial. Try this meditation first thing in the morning upon awakening or last thing at night before falling asleep. You can even try it with eyes open if you're stuck in morning traffic.

> Go inside and visualize your internal boardroom. Imagine your Confident Self sitting at the head of the table. Remembering that curiosity is the gateway to your Confident Self, look around the boardroom, taking an inventory of which of your parts might be around the conference table today. Notice with the same curiosity you'd use when you peek inside a closet or attic, wondering what sorts of stuff you've accumulated over the last five years.

Tension or worry might be there. You might notice control or judgment. Simply notice and acknowledge each part as you scan around the table. Don't try to get rid of or change a part, and don't try to fix the situation. All parts are welcome. You can also check in with each part that you notice and ask what's up with it to see if it has any concerns. Sometimes curiosity expands into a sense of clarity about what's going on internally, or a feeling of calm and possibly even compassion for the part.

The Parts Convention Meditation

The following meditation can help you feel a connection with your Confident Self. Get comfortable in a relaxed position and in a quiet place where you can put yourself fully into this meditation. You may want to put this meditation on tape with soft music and play it back or have a friend guide you through it.

Focus on your breathing. Take a few deep breaths, letting all the tension leave your body. Stay connected with your breathing. Take a deep breath and imagine breathing in curiosity. As you exhale, soak in the curiosity, letting it spread to every cell of your body. Take another deep breath and breathe in curiosity about what's inside of you. Exhale, feeling your body relax again. Feel the tension leaving your body and calmness sweeping over you. Just drink in the sweetness of that calmness.

Imagine that you are standing on a convention stage in an auditorium, looking out at all your parts that have come here today to hear what you have to say. Holding your curiosity, take a few minutes to notice which of your parts are sitting in the audience. Acknowledge each part. And as you do so, pay special attention to where each part is seated. Orchestra? Balcony? Mezzanine? Is there a part or parts way in the back? Or are there parts standing off to the side? Just notice.

The theme of your message is ALL PARTS ARE WELCOME. As you deliver this message, notice how each part receives it. ALL PARTS ARE WELCOME.

It's important to let each part respond in its own natural way, while you curiously watch and learn. Is any part riveted on your every word? Is one falling asleep? Does one roll its eyes? Are parts applauding? Or shaking their heads with irritation at what they hear?

Now see if you can appreciate all the hard work each of your parts has done for you. Notice any parts that have gotten an equal voice or others that have been disenfranchised. Recognize the contributions of as many of your parts as you can and let compassion fill your heart for the protection they have provided. Feel the compassion now, soaking it in from head to toe. Just drink it in.

Notice as you speak to your parts whether you are watching yourself standing at the podium or you are actually standing there looking out. If you are watching yourself, then find the part that's afraid to let you stand alone and ask it to relax and return to its seat. If it won't, then spend time exploring its concerns. As you continue to stand in front of the audience, notice whether you are thinking anything at all. If you are, ask those thoughts to take their seats so that you increasingly become pure awareness. Check periodically as you continue to see if you are thinking, and, if you are, gently send the thoughts back to their seats. As each part returns to its seat, notice what happens to your body and mind. Notice the amount of space you sense and the kind of energy that flows.

Now ask yourself "Who is standing at the podium?" Then notice it's your Self, the one born to run your life. Immerse yourself into this place of Self. Bathe in your confidence, courage, and creativity, feeling them infiltrate every cell of your body.

As you again look out over the convention floor at your parts, notice your sense of connectedness to each one, while at the same time staying centered in your Confident Self. Standing in the center of yourself is standing in your very own curiosity, compassion, confidence, courage, creativity, calmness, clarity, and connectedness. This is who you really are.

Now bathing in all these true qualities of your Confident Self, thank your parts for their support—for being out there on the front lines every day advocating for you. Then in any way you want and in your own time, start bringing your awareness back into the room. Feel the seat beneath you. Hear the sounds around you. Take your time, and when you're ready, open your eyes, bringing all your Confident Self qualities with you back into the room.

Charting the Confident Life

The graph in Figure 2.1 on page 38 helps you chart the qualities of a Confident Life. Choose one of the 8 "C" words *most* present in your life today. Above that "C" word draw a vertical line which will be the highest line in the graph. Next consider the "C" word that is *least* present in your life today. Above that word, draw a vertical line that will be the lowest line in the graph. Then fill in the remaining six lines that are present in your life today in proportion to the highest and lowest. The final profile gives you a picture of which of the eight states of consciousness you can cultivate for a more Confident Life.

Figure 2.1: You and Your Eight "C's"

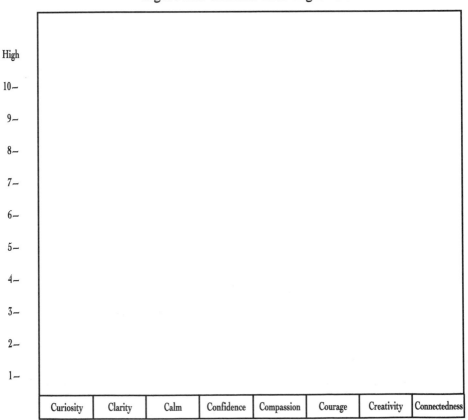

Chapter Three

The Practice of Perception

*Freeing yourself from negative illusions
of the past that eclipse who you really are*

M en are disturbed not by things, but by the
views which they take of them.

—Epictetus

Perceptual Illusions

 I once spent three weeks in Asia, where I immersed
myself in the rich Eastern culture—the spiritual practices,
mesmerizing sights and sounds, and exotic smells and tastes
of food. Upon my return to the United States, I found myself
still immersed in the ways of the East. Shortly thereafter, I

walked into a colleague's office and noticed a book on her desk. My eyes picked up half of the book title, which registered in my brain as "Tea-Ching."

Still basking in the enthusiasm of my trip, I pointed to the book and exclaimed, "Oh, I see you have an interest in Asian culture, too!"

She looked at me as if I were crazy and said, "No. I've never been there and have no desire to go, really."

I took a closer look at the book and chuckled to myself when my eyes caught the complete title, *Teaching in the Elementary Schools.* My Asian frame of reference caused me to create a mind-set about this woman that was really about my mind-set—it was an illusion, not the reality. This illusion, derived from my Asian experience, caused me to frame a new situation in a certain way, eclipsing the objective truth. This minor incident is an example of how we live our daily lives— bringing our past mind-sets to new situations, filtering fresh new experiences, and creating illusions in the present.

One of the universal truths is that the world as we have perceived it—including our perceptions of ourselves—is not the way we are or the world is at all. The Practice of Perception says that our reality is not reality but a subjective reality created in our minds. Psychologist Kurt Lewin's field theory holds that if you believe you are unworthy, unlikable, or ugly—even though others do not perceive you that way— your impression that "I am an undeserving person" is still a fact inside your mind. This illusion influences your behavior as much as if it were objectively true. Field theory says that we do not behave on the basis of objective reality but on the basis of what we perceive to be true, whether our impressions match objective reality or are illusions. Eckhart Tolle has referred to the ego as the illusory sense of self. Albert Einstein called it "an optical illusion of consciousness."

To show how the mind frames new experiences, scientists at Cambridge University conducted experiments with newborn cats in which they restricted the visual field of the kittens to only horizontal lines. Never having seen vertical lines in their early years, the adult cats could recognize horizontal lines (——) but not vertical ones (|). They could jump on tabletops but would routinely bump into the vertical table legs. Vertical lines were not part of the adult cats' mind-set because they had never experienced them as kittens. The point of the experiment was to say that, because of their restricted past, what the cats saw in the present was an illusion.

In regard to confidence, this demonstrates that it is a perceptual illusion to think that control, anger, judgment, and other parts of ourselves are all of who we are. The ways in which we are shaped to perceive the world are what determine our mental outlooks. Beginning in our early years and continuing onward, confidence—or the lack of it—is a mind-set formed from the words we hear and the attitudes, feelings, and actions of parents and other adults. During childhood, the mind records memories that it carries into the future. These snapshots—good or bad—make up our mind-set,

filtering each present situation and defining how we perceive ourselves and other people and situations. In other
words, we look for the horizontal lines because that's what
was shown to us in childhood.

Consider Glenda, who carried a perceptual illusion of herself for many years. She still remembers an aunt holding her
firmly by her seven-year-old shoulders, looking her squarely
in the eyes, pounding into her brain, "You can *never* wear red
because you're a redhead! You look awful in red! It makes
you look like a fire truck with your red hair." This illusion
dominated Glenda's thinking and behavior for forty years,
and she spent her entire life afraid to wear red. Glenda had
molded her thoughts, feelings, and behaviors around her
aunt's perception. At age forty-seven, although she under-
stands that her aunt's perception was not necessarily shared
by everyone, Glenda still feels uncomfortable wearing red
clothes because the perceptual illusion she acquired in childhood still trumps her confidence in adulthood.

When Stephanie brought home an A– on her seventh-
grade report card, her parents said, "Well, why couldn't that
be an A+?" When she won a writing contest and showed her
dad the story, he said, "They mustn't have had too many
entries to pick yours." Stephanie said at forty-something
that she still lives with this sense of needing to prove something—a perceptual illusion that she's not good enough.

Joe is another example of someone who carried a perceptual illusion of himself, almost to the point of destruction.

His typical morning wake-up call from his father was "Get your lazy ass out of bed!" That message pierced his young brain: he was lazy, no good, and unworthy. He spent the majority of his adult life working himself into the ground, trying to prove his worth and confidence through workaholism that almost killed him. "I'm unworthy" is an illusionary message he carried, pushing him to achieve until he could feel worthy, which never worked because he already was worthy.

Try this exercise: Ask a friend to spend one minute looking around your office or whatever room you're in right now. Ask the friend to list mentally as many items as she can that are blue—perhaps the carpet, wallpaper, bindings on books on shelves, curtains, and sofa. After a minute have her close her eyes and name out loud all the items she can remember that are yellow. Most people go blank and cannot remember any yellow items because they were focused on blue. Your friend might look at you strangely, wondering if you've been sniffing the furniture polish, and say something like "I didn't see any yellow because you told me to look for blue." However, if you had instructed her to see yellow, she would've seen yellow items. Even if there were only a few of them, she would've blocked out everything else to focus on whatever yellow color exists in the room.

The point of this exercise is to demonstrate how we collect evidence to fit with what we believe about ourselves from the time we are very young. Many of the feelings we have about ourselves and others are simply illusions. Children who are told they will never measure up often develop a snapshot of themselves as inadequate, defective, inferior, undeserving, unworthy, or unlovable, and these mind-sets direct them as adults. Sometimes we unwittingly go so far as to collect evidence in the present to fit our snapshots in an effort to confirm our deeply held beliefs.

If you think you cannot do well in a job interview (because you think of yourself as inadequate), then you won't do well. If you think you're inadequate, you'll frame each experience through that belief system and collect evidence to fit with it. Situations that contradict the belief that you're inadequate are ignored, discounted, or minimized or not absorbed as part of your perceptual experience. In these ways, you continue to look for your inadequacies, despite the fact that you are presented every day with a veritable rainbow of confidence-building feedback. Compliments sail over your head. You tell yourself that your successes are flukes and your failures are living proof of how inadequate you really are.

It's All in How You See It

The Practice of Perception is based on the notion that your perspective creates your physical and emotional realities and experience of life. You are what you think you are, and you can change yourself by changing your perspective.

By changing how you look at things, you literally can change the circumstances of your personal life. You can transform hardships and despair into a life of confidence and serenity.

Everything you do is a thought before it is an action. For example, think of something simple that you can draw in less than a minute, such as a stick figure or a flower (your skill as an artist doesn't count). Now draw that in the margin of this page. You have just transformed the idea in your head into a physical reality. For another example, consider that this book started out as an idea in my mind. Now it's a tangible object that you're holding in your hands. If I hadn't believed that I could write this book, you wouldn't be reading it right now because thoughts predetermine action.

Everything you create—from making a cake, to redecorating a room, to finding someone on Match.Com—starts in your mind as a thought. The movie *Star Wars*, Beethoven's Fifth Symphony, the condo on your street, your iPod, your PDA, your plasma TV—all started out as thoughts. Planning to ask someone on a date, confronting a hostile colleague, or asking your boss for a raise also are thoughts before they're actions.

The pictures of reality in our heads are based on perceptions we develop from our upbringing. These pictures or mind-sets develop from our own unique family and cultural experiences. They are not objective reality; rather, they are subjective interpretations of reality, filtered through our eyes. In contemporary U.S. society, for example, we have many words to describe colors — pink, orange, yellow, teal, and so forth — but many societies have far fewer words and, as a result, see fewer colors than we do. Eskimos have many words to describe snow, while the English language has only a few. So the Eskimo thinks about and sees more kinds of snow than English-speaking people do because the Eskimo develops more mental pictures of snow.

In much the same way you develop mental pictures of yourself and the world, these pictures direct your feelings and actions, which cause others to react to you in certain ways. Thus, through limited pictures, you create a cycle of interaction that is self-reinforcing because it directs how you think about yourself, the kinds of relationships you attract and are attracted to, and how healthy your lifestyle is. The Practice of Perception — acting out of the belief that life is governed by illusions that shape your thoughts and actions on a daily basis — can free you from these limitations.

Once you understand that it is your limited view that prevents your life from working, not the reality of the world, you stop reacting and start acting, which expands your understanding of the world. In a nutshell, confidence doesn't come from outside reality; rather, it comes from the inner interpretation of reality that you make through limited mental pictures derived from the past. As long as your life works out to suit you (to match your mental mind-set), there's no problem. But when something happens that doesn't fit with your inner picture or someone doesn't live up to your expectations, you react. In this way, the restricted perspective puts you at the mercy of other people and events, undermining confidence in yourself.

Don't Let Your Mind Stunt Your Growth

Suppose your boss walks by your desk in the office. You smile and nod. She looks straight at you, as if through steel, refusing to acknowledge your presence. You shrink inside, thinking you're in disfavor or trouble. You worry the entire week. You text message a top-notch coworker who shares a similar incident he had with this boss—evidence that perhaps it wasn't personal. At a company social gathering, the boss mentions offhandedly that her husband and some employees have complained in the past that she gets so wrapped up with projects that she's constantly thinking in her head and doesn't notice people around her—more evidence that you were not being singled out. The next week the boss calls you into her office. Your stomach flip-flops. You tremble, but she gives you a glowing performance evaluation—final confirmation not only that she does not hold you in disfavor but that she regards you as a highly valued team member.

The culprit that got you into this worry torment is *mind reading*—a perceptual illusion of a situation based on your belief, not hard facts. If you're like most people, at one time or another you've probably projected what you think others are thinking onto a situation, but the truth is those are *your* thoughts, not theirs. That's what makes it an illusion. The message here is *Don't believe everything you think.*

If your *inner critic* (an ego part) is in the habit of jumping to conclusions at work, at home, or at play, go inside to your internal boardroom, use your curiosity, and ask *"Where's the evidence for this conclusion?"* The more you practice this approach, the less you rely on your perceptual illusions and the more you wait to connect the dots *after instead of before* the hard evidence is in. Sometimes you have to wait for the evidence to show up, as with a performance evaluation. At other times you can get a reality check from friends or coworkers. Sometimes you can ask the person directly for clarification. You'll discover that 90 percent of the time you won't find hard evidence to support your illusions. Finding the hard evidence when you think the worst in an uncertain situation, instead of jumping to conclusions, saves you a lot of unnecessary worry.

Take Marcy, for example. She had a series of panic attacks because she was telling herself that it was only a matter of time until she failed at her real-estate job. She said she felt like a fake and worried that her incompetence would surface and she'd lose her job. I was puzzled by the contradiction between her thoughts and the facts. She'd just received an award and bonus for being a top multimillion-dollar salesperson in her company the previous year. She admitted that others saw her as highly accomplished. Still, she said to me, "At first I felt good about the recognition, but then I realized it was a fluke, and it'll never happen again. So I feel like I'm going down the tubes this year!"

Not only did the evidence in Marcy's life not match her perception of herself—it contradicted it. Yet, instead of rejecting her perception and accepting the facts, her illusion trumped the proof. Unwittingly, Marcy was undermining her confidence by telling herself that she was incapable because that was the conditioned lens through which she looked. If she hadn't interrupted the self-defeating illusion, her success would have been marred by it, and her worst nightmare could have come true. Luckily, she was able to separate enough from the self-defeating voice to realize it was a part. She listened to its concerns so that it felt heard and could relax. Today, she remains one of the top-selling real-estate brokers in her region.

People who lack confidence are looking for that deficiency and constantly finding it in their lives. And because they believe they never achieve enough, perfect is never enough. So they always find themselves feeling badly and working to disprove their negative ideas about themselves. They often bend positive feedback from a boss or spouse to fit with their illusionary lenses, turning positive situations into negative ones.

Julie received her promotion, but it wasn't high enough up the corporate ladder. Steve was named top salesperson of the month, but he hadn't broken the all-time sales record. Phyllis made an A in her MBA course, but she was depressed because it wasn't an A+. All three of these people perceived themselves as failures when, in fact, most people would describe them as successful.

Perceptions That Make You Sizzle in Relationships

Ever wonder why certain situations send you over the edge when you take others in stride? Ever wonder why you snap at your spouse or partner for something he or she says or does, and then you regret it minutes later after the damage is done?

Studies explain why people are unable to control their hair-trigger responses. Emotional reactions come from the limbic system, or the "emotional brain." When this part of the brain registers situations as emotionally threatening, we have a fight-or-flight response. On the inside, our bodies secrete adrenaline, and heart, blood pressure, and respiration rates skyrocket, while on the outside we rant and rave, freeze in fear, or get away.

The limbic system, or "old brain," is the part of the brain that houses old hurts from the past. Present events that trigger these reactions can be keys to ancient hurts—memories of past situations buried deep within your old brain that angered or scared you. The amygdala, a tiny almond-shaped part of the old brain, is believed to be the repository of primitive feelings linked with past events. Situations in the present that are similar to those recorded by the old brain trigger the amygdala, which kicks into survival mode.

Gary Zukav explained how illusions can be learning vehicles when triggered in present-day interactions, if we're willing to step back, separate from them, and see the lessons:

> Each interaction with each individual is part of a continual learning dynamic. When you interact with another, an illusion is part of this dynamic. This illusion allows each soul to perceive what it needs to understand in order to heal. It creates, like a living picture show, the situations that are necessary to bring into wholeness the aspects of each soul that requires healing.[1]

This is illustrated by Mark, sweat dripping from his brow, who had spent the entire day cleaning the house from top to bottom to surprise his high-powered, executive wife. She came home, pointed to a dust bunny in the corner of the room, and, in an attempt to help, said, "Oh, honey, you missed a spot right there." Mark went ballistic, accusing her of criticizing his hard work and yelling that nothing was ever good enough for her.

What Mark eventually understood by paying attention to his outbursts was that he had developed an illusion of himself as inadequate, which became a huge trigger for him. Driven by this illusion as an adult, when someone (his wife, boss, coworkers, friends) criticized him in any way, his amygdala flooded his current "new" emotional experience with an "old" emotional memory, causing him to overreact. The library of his old brain reminded him in a split second of all his boyhood failures, having grown up with critical parents whom he never could please, and he would continue to reexperience his belief that he never could get it right. He eventually realized that if he felt that way in most relationships, it couldn't be everybody else—it had to be partly him. This realization was the key to changing his illusionary lens and healing his soul.

If we think of ourselves or certain situations in a fixed way—that we're unworthy or that a situation is dangerous, for example—we'll take those thought patterns with us in our everyday lives and treat them as facts. We unconsciously superimpose those perceptions, or snapshots, on current-day situations. Richard Schwartz explained the contrast between confident versus under-confident people:

> One reason Self-led people can remain calm and clear in the face of anger is because they trust that no matter what the offended person claims happened, it doesn't mean they are bad or are going to be permanently harmed. We are defensive not because someone is attacking us, but because the attack is likely to provoke our inner self-critics, who in turn trigger the worthlessness and terror we accumulated as children. Whatever slight we receive in the present triggers an echo chamber inside us of all the similar hurts we've accumulated from the past. Contemporary events are not what we

fear—it's the unending reverberations we'll have to endure that scare us. We dread any incident that confirms our worst fears about ourselves.[2]

Suppose you've had two heartbreaking romances. Chances are that you would approach the third with a certain degree of trepidation—a thought pattern that it, too, will be a heartbreaking love affair. Perhaps certain personality types remind you of someone who hurt you in the past. You might catch yourself automatically reacting to such types of people with anger or harsh criticism, as if they were the actual people who originally hurt you. Perceptual illusions can block your *connectivity* to other people.

Jamey is a case in point. One of the things that makes Jamey sizzle is when someone lets her down. She and her friend Edie made dinner plans a month in advance. When Jamey called Edie two days before their date to confirm the time, Edie said she'd forgotten to put it on her calendar and had already made theater plans with someone else. Although Edie felt awful, Jamey's hair-trigger reaction was "I cannot trust that you'll do what you say. I must not be very important to you." Edie's excuse could have been that her house burned down, and the knee-jerk thoughts would have been the same because these reactions came partly from Jamey's illusionary ego, not just from Edie's forgetfulness. The situation triggered Jamey's childhood abandonment by her alcoholic father, who habitually took her to the movies and never came back for her.

Jamey learned at eight years of age that she could not trust adults to do what they said because that was what they demonstrated to her over and over again, and she'd carried that illusion into almost every adult relationship, which left her feeling abandoned by friends and loved ones much of the time. The good news is that Jamey learned not to let those old perceptions get in the way of new relationships. She was able to recognize when old feelings (the illusionary parts) crept into new relationships, to separate from them, and to develop compassionate understanding for why they occurred in the first place.

You can reframe old mental snapshots by paying close attention to when they pop up and prevent you from seeing a current situation as it really is. What you want to do is start noticing people and situations that cause you to sizzle. Instead of automatically reacting, ask yourself what old, familiar feelings the experience is bringing up for you. When you do this, you'll see that it is usually an inner perception (a part) that causes you to sizzle, not the present person or circumstance. This will allow you to see present moments more clearly and untangle from them.

Living the Practice of Perception

We tend unconsciously to carry illusions about ourselves that can block our confidence, which, in turn, can short-circuit our relationships, our health, or our climb up the ladder of success. Untangling from illusions of the past and putting on your "parts detector" can give you a different perspective and help you see the water in which you're swimming.

Untangling Yourself from Illusions of the Past

It is a perceptual illusion to believe that *parts* of you are *all* of who you truly are. Disentangling yourself from your parts will help you discover the rest of you that your parts have clouded out. The good news is that you can untangle yourself from negative perceptions about the past that eclipse the real you and clash with the Confident Life you seek today. Once you begin to separate from the past, you see that you are not the problem, but are separate from it.

Look at the dots in Figure 3.1 on page 56. Which one of the middle dots is bigger? The one surrounded by a circle of large dots? Or the one surrounded by a circle of tiny dots? The answer is they're both the same. This is a perceptual illusion. It's the surrounding dots that fool us into thinking one is larger than the other.

Figure 3.1: Which of the center dots is larger?

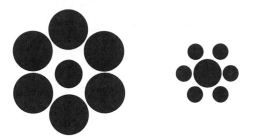

Let's suppose you are the dot in the center of the first drawing in Figure 3.1. Let's say the large dots surrounding you stand for all the parts of you with which you identify: your judgment, anger, criticism, fear, procrastination, and so on. You look smaller surrounded by your parts because they eclipse your Confident Self. Suppose the second drawing illustrates a person who is self-led instead of dominated by parts. The dot in the center surrounded by the circle of small dots looks larger than you, but you're both exactly the same size. You can see this when you look at the center dots in isolation. In other words, standing back and looking objectively at your life helps you separate your Confident Self from parts that you're still carrying with you that undermine your confidence. Although you may have parts that think you are inadequate or unworthy, you begin to realize that the belief is an illusion and not your Confident Self.

Now, look at the square superimposed over the concentric

circles in Figure 3.2. The sides look wobbly and misshapen. This is another perceptual illusion caused by the background. Suppose you are the misshapen square and that the concentric circles in the background represent your parts or ego. When you remove the square from its background, you see that it is perfectly square and not wobbly at all.

Figure 3.2: The background in this figure distorts the square, just as your *parts* can eclipse your *Self-Confidence*

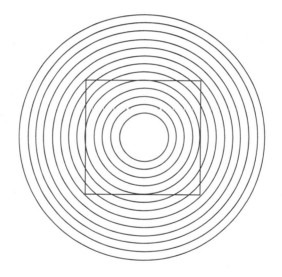

This exercise can help you see the objective truth about yourself: that your negative beliefs are illusions that have eclipsed the real you. This technique can help you separate your mistakes and wrongdoings from yourself. You don't have to become the mistake just because you made one. And you don't have to carry someone else's shame or guilt for something you were not responsible for, either as a child or as an adult in a relationship. The ability to curiously separate yourself from the part of you that is critical, angry, hurt, or sad and to think of these parts as aspects of you instead of all of you allows clarity of perception to emerge.

Putting on Your "Parts Detector"

Make a list of the self-illusions about which you are currently aware. Ask yourself what compliments or affirmations have people consistently given you over the years that you've denied or dismissed? What negative messages did you receive as a child that you can stand back from now and realize that they don't apply to you? What childhood aspirations did you leave standing in the shadows of your life because grownups said you couldn't achieve them? See if you can reclaim ownership of any of the disowned qualities that emerge from this exercise, and put them into practice in your life.

Next, notice how often a part of you pops up with negative predictions. Make a list of these predictions. Beside each negative prediction you list, ask yourself, "Where's the evidence for this prediction?" Not only will you usually find no proof, but you are likely to find that the evidence almost always contradicts the illusions. As you put on your "parts detector," you eventually see that you can no longer count on the illusions to prepare you for the future. Gary Zukav has said that illusions have no power over you when you love, "when *compassion* opens your heart to others, when your *creativity* flows unimpeded joyously into the present moment."[3] This is living from your Confident Self.

Chapter Four

The Practice of Choice

Remembering that you have choices,
from moment to moment, no matter
how difficult the situation

You don't get to choose how you're going to die,
or when. You can only decide how you're going to
live. Now.

—Joan Baez

Maximizing Your Choices

I witnessed firsthand a situation that remains an inspiration for the power of choice in my own life. A concert on
the campus of the University of North Carolina at Charlotte
featured ten Tibetan monks who chanted and danced. I was
impressed with their rhythmic musical instruments, colorful

61

costumes, and ability to chant more than one note simultaneously. More important, I was struck with their gentle nature—their unconditional acceptance of everything that happened without reaction.

These qualities became evident when a group of angry religious fundamentalists gathered outside the auditorium to picket the concert, claiming that Buddhists worshiped idols and that Buddhism was anti-Christian. In protest, they joined hands and sang "Jesus Loves Me." One of the monks came outside to see what was going on. When he witnessed the disturbance, instead of reacting with anger or defensiveness, he approached the circle, joined hands with the protesters, and sang "Jesus Loves Me" with sincerity and respect.

Disarmed by the monk's actions and perhaps realizing they had nothing to fear after all, the group quietly disbanded. My heart was touched by the monk's gentle action. I realized that this was the Practice of Choice in its purest form and saw how much those actions have to offer us in the Western world.

Even more inspiring were the well-publicized struggles of Viktor Frankl, a World War II concentration camp survivor. In his book *Man's Search for Meaning*, Frankl detailed his confinement and brutal treatment at Auschwitz and other Nazi camps.[1] Separated from his wife, starving, and naked, Frankl was stripped of human dignity. Still, through all the suffering and degradation and the fact that other prisoners were dropping dead around him, Frankl saw choices he could make each day. Alone, starving, and freezing, he was convinced that, although the Nazis could take away all the outer conditions of his life, they couldn't rob him of his inner resources—his will to live, his inner spirit. So, paradoxically, despite the outer conditions of his life, Frankl was free because he chose to be. This inner freedom helped him survive the Holocaust, find meaning in his personal tragedy, and rise above his circumstances instead of letting them overpower him. He had decided to choose life instead of letting it choose him.

The actions of the Buddhist monk and Viktor Frankl are reminders that no matter how difficult things get in our daily lives, we still have the freedom to choose. The more you have practiced separating your Confident Self from your ego parts and freeing yourself from negative illusions of the past, the more conscious you will be of the choices you have from moment to moment. Instead of letting circumstances make decisions for us, we can pay attention to what we think, how we feel, and how we act. This type of living from the inside out is the Confident Life in action.

You may have seen the bumper sticker "Misery is optional." No, it didn't say "optimal," although that is a choice we can make when ego parts are leading our lives. When the Confident Self is at the helm, though, we are more conscious of our choices and can use unfortunate experiences as opportunities to change our lives for the better.

If you want to get somewhere, you don't sit down—you

take action and move. The more choices available, the scarier it can be. When we're living from our ego parts, avoiding change feels safer than choosing something new: patronizing the same restaurants, holding the same jobs, following the same daily routines, staying in stale relationships. Sameness, though, just for safety's sake, is an ego part of us that is trying its best to protect us from something that feels threatening. Unfortunately, when it leads our lives, it inadvertently limits us and stunts our growth, keeping us from getting our dream job or finding our soul mate, despite the fact that it has the best of intentions.

So, instead of getting pissed off at sameness, see if, after some separation, your Confident Self can connect with it, acknowledge it for its good intentions, and try to have some appreciation and compassion for how hard it works for you. Sameness might relax and let your Confident Self make different choices, while moving you forward, despite facing risks of the unknown and going against fears. The Confident Self can take a new course of action to solve old problems, stop using old ways that don't work, and stop going back to the same people for the same rejections. If something's not working, your Confident Self can do something different. If that doesn't work, when you're Confident-Led, you can persist with another course of action until eventually the problem is resolved.

See if you can practice choosing one thing to do differently, no matter how small. Practice getting out of your rut, taking a different route home from the office, inviting a new colleague to lunch, or facing a new challenge that previously frightened you. These are examples of choices that help you get back to your Confident Life.

Make Life an Adventure to Experience Instead of a Problem to Solve

We can never fully erase problems and mistakes of the past, but our Confident Self can help us choose how we will live our lives in the present. Confidence helps you think of your next big uncertainty as an *adventure to experience* rather than a *problem to solve.* Suppose you meet someone on Match.com and plan your first get-together at Starbucks. You catch an ego part worrying that this person won't be as attracted to you as you are to him or her or that you won't be as attracted as he or she is to you. Because of your uncertainty, your worry part has already forecasted the date as a problem to solve. Setting up a situation as a problem beforehand automatically brings a whole host of negative thoughts with it, as Eckhart Tolle has so aptly put it: "If uncertainty is unacceptable to you, it turns into fear. If it is perfectly acceptable, it turns into increased aliveness, alertness, and creativity."[2]

Using the Practice of Separation reminds you that your Confident Self can choose to think of the date as an adventure without getting attached to the outcome. This choice keeps your mind open to the new experience, stops your worry from jumping to conclusions, and lets the relationship speak for itself before it is written off, allowing your confidence fertile soil in which to grow.

Making choices is automatic, like breathing. We make them every second of our lives without thinking about it. Perhaps you never knew you had a choice before. If you realize that ego parts—even though they have positive intentions—try to protect you from further hardships in your life, your Confident Self can choose happiness from now on. If your life is not the way you'd like it to be, you can change it by realizing that you have choices, even in situations where you think you don't, and you can make conscious choices.

Even not making a choice is a choice. Ask yourself what choices your ego parts have been making that you were not aware of until now. The more you start making conscious choices in your life, the more confident and happier you'll be.

Acting Versus Reacting

How many times have you found yourself engaged in an unspoken power struggle with colleagues, sales clerks, public servants, family, or friends and reacted negatively to them?

Years ago I shopped at a local store where I frequently encountered a sales clerk who was gruff and rude. No matter how nice I was, she was still discourteous. I tried smiling or asking her about her day. Nothing worked. One day, fed up with her sour attitude, I snapped back at her, which only aggravated the situation, causing her to shoot me fiery-eyed glances. Of course, her fire just fanned the flames of my own. We were both caught in a negative cycle of reacting, which prevented us from acting from our Confident Selves.

If you ever get caught in an uncomfortable interchange, practice acting instead of reacting. Reacting to situations is a knee-jerk behavior that comes from a triggered ego part of you that eclipses your Confident Self—like the stimulus-response of a test-tube organism that doesn't have the ability to make choices. Reacting, without consciously choosing or even knowing you have choices, is a defensive stance that puts you at the mercy of your circumstances, whereas acting is a proactive stance that puts you in the driver's seat. When you separate from the triggered ego part, you provide a space for your Confident Self to act on your behalf—to make conscious choices that put you in charge of most situations.

Once I realized, with curiosity, that my reactions (ego parts) gave the sales clerk decision-making power over my life, changing her behavior was no longer my goal. Instead, I focused on changing my behavior by engaging my Confident Self in how I wanted to act in that situation. My actions didn't depend on the clerk's treating me a certain way. The awareness that I have internal choices made me calmer, more compassionate, and more in charge of my life. So remember, just because your day goes downhill, it doesn't mean *you* have to.

A therapist once told me that after a client had paid her for a session and left, she noticed he had overpaid her with two one-hundred-dollar bills instead of her one-hundred-dollar fee. She said the thought popped into her head that she could keep the extra hundred dollars and nobody would ever know. But her afterthought was that *she* would know. She chased the client down to the parking lot and returned his extra hundred dollars. This is a great example of practicing choice. An ego part of her said, *I can keep the money and nobody will ever know,* but her Confident Self said, *The money doesn't belong to me, and I want to live with honesty and integrity.*

You, too, have the power to act consistently from your Confident Self no matter how life bends and sways. A kind word diffuses a sour attitude. Calm in the face of hysteria has a soothing effect. Compliments reverse aspersions. In each case, your behavior can turn around the tone of a situation. Try looking with curiosity (not judgment) at your small, daily power struggles, and remember: just because you're feeling or thinking something doesn't mean you have to react from it. Notice whether you're wandering through life mindlessly reacting to whatever befalls you or making active choices from your Confident Self, regardless of your life conditions. In other words, ask yourself if you're reacting like a single-celled organism or acting like a human being. Try the four steps below to help you act from the inside out instead of reacting from the outside in.[3]

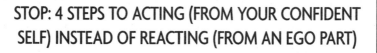

STOP: 4 STEPS TO ACTING (FROM YOUR CONFIDENT SELF) INSTEAD OF REACTING (FROM AN EGO PART)

See inside that a part of you is being triggered. Once you recognize it,

Terminate your usual reaction by stepping back and taking a breath.

Open a dialogue with the part of you that is triggered and, with *curiosity,* see if it will relax and let you handle the situation.

Persist in getting to know the part each time it gets triggered, so that it can relax instead of react.

Good Luck? Bad Luck? Who Knows?

There is a story about a Chinese farmer who had an old horse for tilling his fields. One day the horse escaped into the hills, and when the farmer's neighbors sympathized with the old man over his bad luck, he replied, "Bad luck? Good luck? Who knows?"

A week later the horse returned with a herd of wild horses from the hills, and this time the neighbors congratulated the farmer on his good luck. His reply, again, was "Good luck? Bad luck? Who knows?"

Then when the farmer's son was attempting to tame one of the wild horses, he fell off its back and broke his leg. Everyone thought this was very bad luck. Not the farmer, whose only reply was "Bad luck? Good luck? Who knows?"

Weeks later, the army marched into the village and conscripted every able-bodied man they could find. When they saw the farmer's son with his broken leg, they let him off. Now was that good luck or bad luck? Who knows?

The farmer was a wise man, making active choices about how he would think and act about his life conditions—instead of constantly reacting to life's ups and downs. The farmer knew that blessings often come to us in disguise. This awareness is the bedrock of confidence.

I experienced a similar incident. My most memorable event landing in Sydney, Australia, at 8:00 AM wasn't the famous opera house or the harbor. It was being informed that, out of 350 passengers, I was the only one whose baggage hadn't arrived from Los Angeles. Red-eyed and exhausted after a thirteen-hour flight, those were not the first Aussie words I wanted to hear.

Needless to say, I was heartsick. "Why me, out of all these people?" I groaned. This was bad luck of the worst kind. Or was it? I reminded myself that some blessings masquerade as pain, loss, or disappointment, but standing in the lost-

and-found line I had great difficulty seeing anything positive about that experience. With curiosity, I took a breath and stepped back from the situation in my mind, thinking about the story of the farmer. Sure enough, what had appeared as bad luck turned out to be good luck. The airline gave me one hundred Australian dollars on the spot, and by the time I'd eaten and returned to my hotel, my luggage had arrived. I ended up with all my luggage and an extra hundred dollars to boot. See if you can recall an episode in your life that initially appeared as a problem but turned out to be a boon.

As you apply the Practice of Choice, the way in which you look at your life changes. You begin to feel freer inside and more confident in challenging situations. You don't look through rose-colored glasses, but you no longer see challenges as bleak and bewildering, either. You see more hope than despair, and you see gains, even in loss and disappointment. Practicing this awareness builds your confidence.

Choose Your Life Instead of Letting It Choose You

Ask yourself a few questions. Are you making free choices in your life? Or do you feel like a prisoner of your circumstances? Are you condemned to unhappiness because of the hand life has dealt you? If you discover that your life conditions are controlling you instead of you controlling them, you may feel as though you are in an emotional prison. The power of choice is within you. Connecting with that powerful part of yourself can make you feel more confident in your life. If Viktor Frankl had choices in his hardships, then surely you and I have choices at work, at home, and at play. The Tibetan monk's actions also demonstrate that in the face of adversity, we can choose our actions instead of letting them choose us.

Look at the drawing of the old lady in the picture below. She has a big nose, a scarf on her head, and her long chin is buried in her fur coat. Look at the drawing closely and try to figure out why she is so sad and unhappy.

The Eye of the Beholder

Did you realize that I just guided your perception of this situation in the direction I wanted it to go? The truth is that there is also a young girl in this drawing. I could just have easily guided you to see her instead of the old lady.

Perceptual psychologists have presented this ambiguous drawing of the old/young woman to many research participants. Given the expectation that they would see an old woman, they indeed did find the old woman's face before the young woman's face. Told that they would be shown the face of a young woman, they tended to see the young woman's face first and often had difficulty seeing the image of the old lady.

You can apply the Practice of Choice by going back and reexamining the picture in a new light. This time, as you look at the drawing in a new way, you can see a young woman. The old woman's eye becomes the young woman's ear. The old woman's nose becomes the young woman's jawbone. The old woman's mouth is the young woman's necklace. Now you can look at the same picture and see an entirely different image.

Such is life. When we are Confident-Led, we are more aware of choices and can reexamine our lives and reinterpret what we see. We can choose to focus on good or bad, the happiness or unhappiness, the success or failure. We can perceive our life conditions as roadblocks and let them stand in our way or as stepping-stones from which to learn lessons. If you have filtered your life up until now through a negative lens of the past, you can ask your eyes, ears, and other senses if they would be willing to look for the beauty, joy, fun, and happiness in life.

This will allow you to see your life in a different way, from fresh new angles, and to watch your life transform around you—to see what was always there that you never noticed before.

Looking at Your Life Through Fresh Eyes

When I first set foot in Venice, I was dazzled by the beauty and culture—the aroma and flavor of Italian food, the priceless antiquities, the slope and design of the ancient buildings, and the romantic gondolas floating in the canals to the sounds of Old World music. On the second day, I started to notice cracks in the pavement and buildings and how hot and dusty it was. The next day I noticed garbage floating in the canals and graffiti marring the buildings that I'd passed many times but hadn't noticed before. After a few more days, I'd had my fill of Italian food, and the music had become old hat. By the end of the week, Venice had soured, and I was ready to go home.

How many times have you started a vacation excited about a new place only to find that you have a whole different feeling about it when it's time to leave? The place didn't change—you did. Venice was still the same romantic, beautiful place when I left that it was when I arrived. All that changed was my view of it. Since it was only my view that had changed, that means I could have changed it back by looking at the place through fresh eyes.

Many times, as we become familiar with our routines, we lose the fresh outlook we once had. Rarely do we maintain the exhilaration of our first romantic relationship or the enthusiasm with which we began parenthood. It is easy to become bored with the everyday monotony of life. We chug Red Bulls and Starbucks to get through pressure-cooker days. We shake our fists at the heavens when the Internet is down or our PDAs aren't moving fast enough. We get mired in daily ruts, and life loses its glow. The thrill and wonder might seem to have vanished, and we might feel as if we've seen and done it all. This is only a mental outlook that can change. This change, in turn, creates more positive feelings and a new experience of your life.

If you could view your life through the fresh eyes of a foreigner, would you see the drudgery of another day's work and unpaid bills or the freshness and richness of your life? Try this simple exercise. The next time you go to work, use the Practice of Separation described in Chapter 2. Imagine you have entered your workplace for the very first time. Look at people and places around you as if you have never seen them before and are appreciating them for the first time. Notice what hangs on walls, smell the flowers on someone's desk, see the color of the blouse or jacket a colleague is wearing, pay attention to the colors of the floor or the architecture of the buildings on the same street. Be mindful of the eyes of a coworker, subordinate, or boss. Look into and behind their eyes. What do you notice there? Be aware of what you're thinking and feeling inside.

You will discover a world that you haven't seen before. The

philosopher Pierre Teilhard de Chardin described this technique as "ever more perfect eyes in a world in which there is
always more to see." As you practice this approach, you'll
start to tap the power within you to change your life. The key
is to get in the habit of looking at yourself and everything you
do in a different way and, when you see it differently, to
change your outlook again. All of us have the power to
change the views we take of ourselves and of the daily world
in which we live. You can begin to exercise that power now
by choosing a different outlook on yourself and your life.

Living the Practice of Choice

You have the power to change your daily world (both
inside and outside) by the view you take of it. You can redis-
cover those two worlds that you have lived in for so long and
see them with new insights and greater clarity.

Choosing to Befriend Your Worry

Are you wigged out about the outcome of something that
hasn't even happened yet? In the next few days, determine
if you're worrying about an upcoming problem you're facing
at work, with a family member, or with a friend. Suspend
your judgment and be curious about the thoughts, feelings,
and body sensations that bubble up inside about the challenge.[4] Using the separation process in Chapter 2, follow

these six steps and see if they help you with your worry part:

1. **Find** your worry.
2. If you can, **focus** all your attention on it.
3. Notice how you **feel** toward the worry part.
4. If you feel any of the "C" words described in Chapter 2 (your Confident Self), **befriend** the worry—see if you can get to know the worry, offer appreciation for its intention, and establish relationship between your Confident Self and the worry part.
5. If the response to step 3 is another part (such as judgment or frustration), ask the part if it would be willing to step aside. If so, continue to step 6. If not, go back to step 3 until more of the Confident Self (any of the "C" words) is present.
6. What are the worry's **fears** or concerns? The worry might say something like "I'm afraid I'll do poorly in the job interview." The mere presence of the Confident Self as it connects with the worry—making friends with it instead of trying to get rid of it—can generate calm, compassion, and courage within.

Remember, your ego parts are always trying to help you in their own way, even when it might not seem like it to you. Developing a relationship with your parts and trying to understand and appreciate their roles in your life—instead of ignoring them or pushing them away—is the hallmark of the Practice of Choice.

Making Conscious Choices

Making conscious choices puts us in the position of leading life with confidence. On what choices, left to chance or another person, could you take action? The exercise below can help you reclaim the power in your life by taking action from the perspective of your Confident Self on matters you unwittingly may have left to chance. In the first column, name a hardship in your life. In the second column, describe what you would like to accept about the situation. In the third column, identify aspects about the situation that your Confident Self can choose. I have given you two examples to get you going.

RECLAIMING THE POWER IN YOUR LIFE		
The Problem	**I Can Accept**	**I Can Choose**
1. My job sucks	I can adjust my attitude as long as I'm working there.	To focus on the benefits of the job to see if that makes a difference before calling it quits
2. My colleague is a negative person.	I cannot change her.	I can be a positive person regardless of how she thinks.

Chapter Five

The Practice of Optimism

*Looking for the positive, instead of
the negative, even in the most
challenging situations*

'Twixt the optimist and pessimist the difference is
droll: The optimist sees the doughnut but the pessimist sees the hole.

—*McLandburgh Wilson*

Are You an Optimist or Pessimist?

here once was a woman who woke up one morning, looked
in the mirror, and noticed she had only three hairs on her head.
"Well," she said, "I think I'll braid my hair today." So she did
and she had a wonderful day.

The next day she woke up, looked in the mirror, and saw that she
had only two hairs on her head.

"Hmm," she said, "I think I'll part my hair down the middle today." So she did, and she had a grand day.

The next day she woke up, looked in the mirror, and noticed that she had only one hair on her head.

"Well," she said, "Today I'm going to wear my hair in a ponytail." So she did, and she had a fun, fun day.

The next day she woke up, looked in the mirror, and noticed that there wasn't a single hair on her head.

"Yeah!" she exclaimed. "I don't have to fix my hair today!"

This woman's ability to remain positive when confronted with challenges illustrates the Practice of Optimism. Psychiatrist David Burns says that bad feelings about ourselves, our relationships, and our lives in general come from pessimistic thoughts.[1] Our ego parts take over the internal boardroom of our lives—often when we don't even realize it—and unconsciously filter out the positive aspects of our lives and infuse their own. Parts such as anxiety, depression, short-temperedness, or anger filter their past concerns through the present. Without an awareness and presence of the Confident Self, it is easy to succumb to pessimistic and hopeless parts of ourselves, especially if it has been part of our history. Pessimism makes flaws stand out from the shine, successes seem more like failures. Looking through the lens of the negative and filtering out the positive contributes to the belief that very little in our lives is working correctly.

Welcoming All Your Parts

When an ego part pops up inside of us, we typically have another part that gets triggered. For example, if I'm about to ask my boss for a raise, tension might appear at my internal boardroom table to say "I'm nervous," which could trigger another part such as judgment, which might say something like "Stop being such a wuss!" Or frustration or even anger could speak up and say something like "Damn it! You've been putting this off long enough!"

Our ego parts are always trying to protect us in their own way, as when a reflexive eye blink protects the eye from a foreign object suddenly flying toward it. In the example I just gave, tension might be trying to warn me that a threat is out there somewhere. Judgment might be trying to give me the courage not to be nervous. And frustration and anger might be giving me a good kick in the pants so that I will take the action to get that raise. They are struggling among themselves because each wants a voice in how to solve the dilemma.

The Practice of Optimism embodies looking for the deeper intent of each of your ego parts while remembering that there is no such thing as a bad part. You are living the Practice of Optimism when you try to understand how each part that pops up inside is trying to protect you, not hurt you. Try welcoming all your parts and listening to their different points of view. See if you can listen to them as if they are individual people inside you. You will start to get more and more of a sense that your parts are speaking and that it is your Confident Self who is listening and who will take the leadership in asking for the raise and making sure all your needs are met, too.

A colleague of mine loved the warm, long days of summer but hated the cold, short days of winter. One day in June on the longest day of the year, I said to her, "You must be on cloud nine!" "No, I'm feeling down," she replied, "because tomorrow the days start getting shorter again."

I couldn't believe my ears. She'd looked forward to that day all year long. Now it had arrived, but she couldn't fully enjoy it because she was already thinking about the short days of winter coming. When I pointed that out, she wasn't even conscious that an ego part of her had hijacked her leadership and taken over her internal boardroom. She was able to acknowledge the part, thanked it for the protection it offered, and asked it to step back. This process allowed a more positive outlook to emerge. In other words, her Confident Self was back in the driver's seat.

Pessimism is actually a type of black-and-white thinking. How pessimistic are you? The exercise on page 84 tests how good you are at looking for the silver lining. From the perspective of the Confident Self, see if you can turn each of the ten pessimistic thoughts into a more balanced one, such as "Life does contain problems, and there are also solutions to those problems, so I can focus on the solutions." Try to reword the statements genuinely, in ways that are truthful for you. In the future, catch the part of yourself sending rigid

READER/CUSTOMER CARE SURVEY

HEFG

We care about your opinions! Please take a moment to fill out our online Reader Survey at **http://survey.hcibooks.com**.
As a **"THANK YOU"** you will receive a **VALUABLE INSTANT COUPON** towards future book purchases
as well as a **SPECIAL GIFT** available only online! Or, you may mail this card back to us.

First Name _____ MI. _____ Last Name _____

Address _____ City _____

State _____ Zip _____ Email _____

1. Gender
- ☐ Female ☐ Male

2. Age
- ☐ 8 or younger
- ☐ 9-12 ☐ 13-16
- ☐ 17-20 ☐ 21-30
- ☐ 31+

3. Did you receive this book as a gift?
- ☐ Yes ☐ No

4. Annual Household Income
- ☐ under $25,000
- ☐ $25,000 - $34,999
- ☐ $35,000 - $49,999
- ☐ $50,000 - $74,999
- ☐ over $75,000

5. What are the ages of the children living in your house?
- ☐ 0 - 14 ☐ 15+

6. Marital Status
- ☐ Single
- ☐ Married
- ☐ Divorced
- ☐ Widowed

7. How did you find out about the book?
(please choose one)
- ☐ Recommendation
- ☐ Store Display
- ☐ Online
- ☐ Catalog/Mailing
- ☐ Interview/Review

8. Where do you usually buy books?
(please choose one)
- ☐ Bookstore
- ☐ Online
- ☐ Book Club/Mail Order
- ☐ Price Club (Sam's Club, Costco's, etc.)
- ☐ Retail Store (Target, Wal-Mart, etc.)

9. What subject do you enjoy reading about the most?
(please choose one)
- ☐ Parenting/Family
- ☐ Relationships
- ☐ Recovery/Addictions
- ☐ Health/Nutrition
- ☐ Christianity
- ☐ Spirituality/Inspiration
- ☐ Business Self-help
- ☐ Women's Issues
- ☐ Sports

10. What attracts you most to a book?
(please choose one)
- ☐ Title
- ☐ Cover Design
- ☐ Author
- ☐ Content

TAPE IN MIDDLE; DO NOT STAPLE

BUSINESS REPLY MAIL
FIRST-CLASS MAIL   PERMIT NO 45   DEERFIELD BEACH, FL

POSTAGE WILL BE PAID BY ADDRESSEE

Health Communications, Inc.
3201 SW 15th Street
Deerfield Beach FL 33442-9875

FOLD HERE

Comments

messages and befriend it using the six steps presented in Chapter 4. Then see if the part can relax and view the situation from a more optimistic vantage point. After a period of dedicated practice, you'll most likely see a difference in your ability to think and feel more positively about yourself.

Who's Zooming Who?

One year at tax season a wealthy client stormed into my office, cursing and waving his hands. Without saying hello, he slammed into the sofa. When I asked him what was wrong, he said, "I made more money than I've ever made in my life." "That's great!" I exclaimed, realizing he'd made more money in one year than some people make in a lifetime. "Wonderful? The hell you say!" he sneered, "I've gotta come up with a half million dollars in taxes!"

Here was a man so caught up in his loss that it overshadowed his gains. He'd lost sight of his abundance and was resentful that he had to pay a small portion to the Internal Revenue Service. Unfortunately, this very rich man continued to live an impoverished life because the pessimistic part of him was in charge of his internal boardroom.

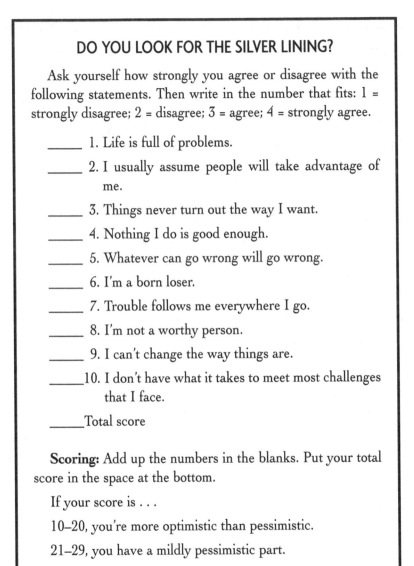

DO YOU LOOK FOR THE SILVER LINING?

Ask yourself how strongly you agree or disagree with the following statements. Then write in the number that fits: 1 = strongly disagree; 2 = disagree; 3 = agree; 4 = strongly agree.

_____ 1. Life is full of problems.

_____ 2. I usually assume people will take advantage of me.

_____ 3. Things never turn out the way I want.

_____ 4. Nothing I do is good enough.

_____ 5. Whatever can go wrong will go wrong.

_____ 6. I'm a born loser.

_____ 7. Trouble follows me everywhere I go.

_____ 8. I'm not a worthy person.

_____ 9. I can't change the way things are.

_____10. I don't have what it takes to meet most challenges that I face.

_____Total score

Scoring: Add up the numbers in the blanks. Put your total score in the space at the bottom.

If your score is . . .

10–20, you're more optimistic than pessimistic.

21–29, you have a mildly pessimistic part.

30–40, you have a strong pessimistic part.

This form of pessimism is called *zoom-lens thinking,* and it promotes the picture that *I'm not enough, and I don't have enough, and there never will be enough.* Pessimism acts like a zoom lens, zeroing in and magnifying the negative aspects of a situation while clouding out the positive aspects. Zooming can make you feel like your life sucks, despite the fact that others around you might think you have a charmed life. When you zoom yourself, you feel like a perpetual failure even when you're successful. Parts of you do the zooming; your Confident Self uses a wide-angle lens.

Zooming sabotages our lives in a big way when a part compares us to the top in each field—standards so high that one human being could never reach them all: the wealth of Donald Trump, the sex appeal of Angelina Jolie, the gumption of Judge Judy, the wit of Ellen DeGeneres, the compassion of Mother Teresa, and on and on.

Zoom-lens thinking gives you the illusion that others have what you don't. When you use someone else's life as a yardstick to evaluate your own, you judge yourself unfairly and come out on the short end of the stick. It also blocks out the talents and skills that you do possess. Even if you excelled in three out of four areas, the pessimistic part ignores the three areas of success and zooms in on the one where you fall short. This feeling of lack, when focused on, expands and creates lack even when abundance is all around you. This distortion prevents you from seeing your Confident Self and makes your life feel empty and lacking—even when you're viewed as outstanding by others.

Another form of zooming turns compliments into dispersions. When feedback conflicts with the image of ourselves, we change it to fit our pessimistic thoughts by discounting it, ignoring it, downplaying it, or distorting it in some way. The Chinese philosopher Huang Po said, "The foolish reject what they see, not what they think; the wise reject what they think, not what they see."

When someone told Grace how nice her new haircut looked, she said, "Are you kidding? This old mop?" When friends complimented her on her artwork, she snapped, "Are you making fun of me? I know I'm not as creative as you, but I'm doing the best I can." Grace saw only the worst in herself and could not affirm the good.

Do you blush when someone praises you? Do you feel discomfort when you're applauded for a kind deed? Do you feel awkward when someone compliments you on how you look? Compliments are sometimes hard to accept, especially when you cannot acknowledge the good in yourself. You may find it easier to accept negative comments and put-downs because they more closely match the parts of you that run your life. Many of us, because we are so used to criticism, feel more comfort with it than praise, but that's not the whole truth about who we are.

It has been said that the first and worst of all frauds is to cheat oneself. Self-deception is the inability to see the bigger picture, as if we looked through the objective eyes of an outsider. It causes us to deny ourselves the same loving-kindness and self-respect that we give to others. We're usually unaware that we go about our days collecting evidence of our flaws like we're catching butterflies in a net. It is important to be aware of and acknowledge mistakes and human limitations, but for an honest assessment of yourself it's also important to balance your shortcomings with your "tallcomings." Seeing yourself truthfully requires that you put on your wide-angle lens and name the good things about yourself, too. You can overcome self-deception by acknowledging your strong points and imperfections, by not putting yourself down, and by treating yourself with the same respect you give to others.

Ask yourself if you're more comfortable living the life of an underdog than you are living on top. Are you so accustomed to struggle and heartache that you're uncomfortable with profit and happiness? If so, ask yourself with curiosity which parts are zooming your life, eclipsing your Confident Self. Next, stand back and pay attention to the kinds of evidence that you collect during a day about yourself. Humility is the loving truth about yourself. Do you focus on the all-too-familiar shortcomings? Or do you hold out for the "tallcomings" that give you equally honest feedback about who you are? As a way of seeing the truth about yourself, try accepting compliments into your heart without false pride or false modesty and accepting compliments graciously—instead of dismissing them or letting them sail over your head.

When a business associate compliments your work in a sales meeting, it would be great if you could say confidently, "Thank you. I'm glad you appreciate my hard work on the project," instead of, "Oh, it was no big deal. Anybody could have done it." You will feel more connected and more confident within yourself, and you'll present yourself in a more confident way.

Look for the Diamond in the Rough

The Confident Life gives you the awareness that you have choices and the capacity to see a given situation from a variety of perspectives. The way we choose to look at situations, not the conditions themselves, determines our happiness and peace of mind. This fundamental truth, which has endured throughout the ages, has been taught for centuries by philosophers, spiritual leaders, psychologists, and even management consultants. Once you can see a situation from more than one standpoint, your confidence gets stronger and becomes greater than the outer strength, thus ruling in most circumstances.

This is the Practice of Optimism. Like two sides of a coin, every situation contains good and bad; you can look at the positive side or the negative side. You can see the gains in the losses, the beginnings in the endings. When you hit forty, you can think of it as half a life left or as half a life over. When you enter a rose garden, you can be drawn by the beauty and fragrance of the flowers or be repelled by the thorns. When you hear the weather forecast of 50 percent chance of rain, you can realize that there's also a 50 percent chance that it won't rain. You can always find the granule of good in the bad when you look for it: more beauty than flaws, more hope than despair, more blessings than disappointment. Once you realize that things happen as they are supposed to happen, you can start to accept every situation at face value and know that some good is being born. This idea of holding on to the belief that something good will come out of adversity is illustrated by one of Nasrudin's adventures:

Nasrudin and his master were hunting in the forest. The master cut his thumb while shooting his bow and arrow because he held them incorrectly. Nasrudin stopped the bleeding and bandaged the deep wound as his master moaned in pain. In an attempt to console his master, Nasrudin said, "Sir, there are no mistakes, only lessons, and we can learn from them if we're willing."

The master became enraged. "How dare you lecture me!" he barked.

And with that he threw Nasrudin into a deserted well and continued on without his devoted servant.

A little farther on, a group of forest people captured the master and took him to their chief for human sacrifice. The fire was roasting hot, and the master was about to be thrown into it when the chief noticed his bandaged thumb and set him free. It was a rule that all sacrificial victims had to be perfect specimens. Realizing how right Nasrudin had been, the master rushed back to the well and rescued his faithful servant. Acknowledging his unjust actions, the master pulled Nasrudin out and asked him for forgiveness for the terrible mistake he'd made.

Nasrudin assured him that he had not made a mistake at all. On the contrary, he insisted that another lesson was concealed here. Nasrudin told his master that he had done Nasrudin a great service by throwing him into the well. He thanked his master for saving his life, explaining that if he had continued with him into the forest, the forest people would have taken him for sacrifice and surely he would have died.

"You see," Nasrudin said, "there are no mistakes, only lessons to learn. What we call our mistakes can be blessings in disguise, if we're willing to learn from them."

This time the master smiled and nodded in agreement.

There will be times when you may forget, make a mistake, or say or do something wrong. When you are Confident-Led, however, you are able to bring compassion, instead of condemnation, to the parts that screwed up and the courage to amend it. This helps you turn your mistakes into lessons and figure out what you can learn about yourself from them. This Practice of Optimism can contribute to your personal and career success. Thinking of mistakes and failures as lessons can keep you in an optimistic frame of mind and keep the discouraged and hopeless parts of yourself from taking over. Mistakes viewed as lessons (open-ended curiosities) build confidence and success; mistakes viewed as failures (close-ended judgments) undermine confidence and success. Turning mistakes into lessons—by simply reframing your life conditions—is another way to build yourself up instead of tear yourself down.

We also can apply this approach to how we look at the people in our lives. I believe most people are doing the best they can most of the time. When we look beneath the surface of our judgments (the ego) and stretch to see people's motives, it can soften our reactions. A friend of mine was mad at her husband because he wanted her to keep her cell phone with her so he could reach her during the day. She felt his request was unreasonable, that he was being controlling. Yet when she discussed the matter with him, he explained that it was his way of staying connected to her and showing his love. The ability to see beneath the surface of her husband's actions and focusing on his motives melted her heart toward him. In the same vein, the Practice of Optimism helps us see beneath the surface of our ego parts, which gives us a deeper understanding of their motives, softens our feelings toward them, and provides more inner connectedness, compassion, and calm.

An office manager, an ego-driven fault finder, went to great lengths to create defeat in his subordinates. The more inept they looked, the more competent he felt. He seemed more secure and in charge when things fell apart or when an employee made a mistake. You could see the relief on his face when someone in the office hit a dead end. He would swell up like a frog and throw his weight around, but when someone handled a job well or figured out a computer problem that had the rest of the staff stumped, the office manager seemed to feel uncomfortable and agitated. Everyone in the office despised this man who, driven by his own insecure ego parts, used his authority to disguise his own inferiority.

Underneath the "puffed-up frog" was a "scared little toad."

Once we are able to look beneath the surface parts of others and spot their vulnerable parts, it gives us empathy for them and deeper insight into ourselves. Compassion for others and ourselves allows us to more easily see our daily reality as lessons with which we can choose optimistic action instead of pessimistic reaction.

One of the great paradoxes of life is the realization that people and situations that upset you often have the most to offer for developing your confidence. They can provide you with an opportunity to change yourself, if you're willing to look at it that way. Try to look at coworkers who upset you as messengers or teachers who are present to help you learn more about yourself. Just as the master was doing a great service for Nasrudin by throwing him in the well, some people you might think of as enemies might be your best allies. Those who anger you, embarrass you, hurt you, con-tradict you, and—yes—even betray you might be doing you a great favor by bringing you lessons that can make you stronger and more confident so you can successfully meet the next challenge that comes your way.

Although it can be a challenge to find the diamond in the rough, it gets easier with practice. You can pinpoint the challenge contained in each "negative" experience and ask yourself, *What can I manage or overcome here?* and *How can I turn this situation around to my advantage?* Start to make it a goal to use every experience—no matter how painful or difficult, big or small—as a lesson from which to grow. Change the labels you apply to situations so that the new labels put hardship into a more positive and workable light. Try to create a no-lose, no-victim situation, and you will notice that the winning vantage point will empower you to live each day with greater confidence.

Want What You Have
Instead of Have What You Want

There was a time, when I got together with certain wealthy friends of mine, that their conversations revolved around acquiring something new and different. First it was a new swimming pool, and for months their conversations, thoughts, and behaviors were centered on the planning and building of the pool. Ever since it was built, it has rarely been mentioned and hardly ever used. Instead, they moved on to focus on a completely new project of building a mountain home. Blueprints, fabric, and landscaping were the talk in months to come. Next it was two or three expensive cars, a new guest house, and a new beach bungalow. The mountain home was practically never inhabited and was eventually sold so they could buy a place in the Caribbean and travel the world. Both of them told me they were deeply unhappy with themselves and each other and couldn't figure out why. They hoped to find contentment in the material things they could afford and the exotic places they could go, but they never did. As far as I know, they are still traveling the world and searching.

When we think of an optimistic life only in terms of what we want, we are operating from a position of lack and discontent. The ego parts focus on what is missing from our lives, and the mind is fooled into thinking that more of something or someone will fill that void and make us complete. Although these ego parts are to be commended for their well-intended efforts to get for us what we don't have, the truth is that whatever we focus on expands. When *want* and *desire* take over as CEOs of our internal boardroom, we are literally seeing our lives through the eyes of lack, and since that increases the feeling that our lives are lacking, we want more and more to satisfy the hunger. Want and desire are bottomless pits. They hang out on the sidelines—pushing us to overspend, overeat, and overindulge—and indulging our wants still doesn't fulfill us because a day or week later we must have something else.

The Dalai Lama says in his book *The Art of Happiness*, "The true antidote of greed is contentment. If you have a strong sense of contentment [that is, if you are more Confident-Led], it doesn't matter whether you obtain the object or not; either way, you are still content."[2] He says there are two ways to reach contentment. One is to acquire everything we want and desire: an expensive house, sporty car, perfect mate, gourmet foods, fashionable clothes, exotic trips, perfectly toned body. The problem with this is that sooner or later there will be something we want that we can't have. The second and more reliable approach is to want and feel grateful for what we already have, interpreted here to mean that we are living through the eyes of our Confident Self, who is seated at the head of our internal boardroom table. You already have everything you need for an optimistic life. It starts when you want what you already have instead of insisting that you have what you want, like the old woman who, looking for her eyeglasses, realized they were on her nose the whole time.

An Attitude of Gratitude: Rx for Pessimism

Eleanor took a hard-earned vacation to a Florida resort. During the entire trip, she complained of the sweltering heat, the grim-faced people, and the long lines. Everything was far too expensive. The music, she complained, sounded like a truckload of socket wrenches being dumped on a radiator. All she wanted was a chair and an air conditioner.

On her last day at the resort, something happened that opened her wide-angle lens. Just beyond the scent of gardenias and jasmine, she saw a woman wearing an oxygen mask and carrying an oxygen tank. She paused for a moment before walking in silence back into the world of glaring sunlight, crowds, and sore feet—this time with no complaints.

Sometimes the trivial and petty things in life distract us

from what is most important, and it takes a jolt to realize how truly fortunate we are. The day-to-day annoyances we complain about are suddenly trivial when we face a major catastrophe. We gripe and complain about minor inconveniences when our lives are already rich and full.

How many times a day do you stop and give thanks for the blessings you have—the food on your table, the shelter over your head, your loved ones who have their health, and the other special people who touch your life? Counting your blessings and being grateful turn pessimism into optimism. This helps you to see the glass as half full instead of half empty and to see the good in everything that comes your way. When you're grateful for what you already have, you can practice reminding the lacking part of you where the abundance lies in your life.

There is another reason for choosing optimism over pessimism, according to physician and mind-body expert Larry Dossey:

> Optimists have more stable cardiovascular systems, more responsive immune systems, and loss of a hormonal response to stress compared to pessimists. They have a stronger sense of self-efficacy, so they're more likely to invoke healthier behavior because they think it can make a difference.[3]

Research also has shown that optimists live happier lives, have fewer health problems, and actually live longer than pessimists. High stress and pessimism also have been linked to other body-chemistry changes that are believed to produce cancerous cells. Negative thoughts and moods cause your body to secrete chemicals that can harm you physically, potentially shortening your life. Optimistic thoughts, on the other hand, can create body chemistry that boosts your immune system by increasing the number of disease-fighting immune cells. In short, optimism leads to increased well-being because it leads you to engage actively in life. Pessimism can make you physically sick and kill you; optimism can heal and sustain you. As you embrace more optimism and joy, you can be healthier, more confident, and live longer.

Living the Practice of Optimism

Optimists don't possess some magical joy juice. They are not smiley-faced romantics living through rose-colored glasses. They are realists who take positive steps to solve problems rather than swimming around in them. You can cultivate optimism through practice—becoming more famil-iar with your parts by understanding them instead of bat-tling with them, reframing your life with a wide-angle lens, and practicing gratitude.

Mapping Your Parts

Mapping your parts can bring you deeper insight into how your ego parts and Confident Self interact on the inside. Think of a situation you've been struggling with lately. Notice all the different parts that come up around that situation. Let's say you're in an intimate relationship, fraught with conflict, and it's weighing you down. Examples of parts that might come up for you might be worry ("I'm afraid we can't work this out"), frustration ("I'm tired of living this way"), fear ("I'm afraid of what my life would be like without you"), or judgment ("If you weren't so self-centered, we wouldn't be having this problem"). Map your parts, using the following steps:

1. Whatever the situation, identify the various parts that come up around it. Don't force anything. Just notice through curiosity.

2. Focus attention on one part. Stay with that part to get a sense of the color, shape, image, or body sensation.

3. Allow the part to show itself by drawing it on a large piece of paper. Draw the part as it looks or feels on the inside of you. You can use crayons, paint, colored pencil, or any other media of your choice.

4. Does the part have a belief? If so, write that belief beside the part.

5. Does the part contain emotions? If so, list them.

6. Stay with that part until another part comes up. Then find the color, shape, image, or physical sensation of that part and draw it on the page.

7. Continue these steps with each new part that comes up for you.

8. Notice which parts are aligned with each other and which ones are polarized on the issue in question.

9. Once all parts around this issue are mapped, ask yourself where your Confident Self is in the mapping scheme.

Putting on Your Wide-Angle Lens

It's best to catch yourself zooming early, before you get too far. Then put on your wide-angle lens and look at the big picture of your life—especially the blind spots your zoom lens shuts out. This can put your Confident Self smack dab in the leadership of your life. A good way to use the wide-angle lens is to identify a complaint you have about your life or yourself. Perhaps your mutual fund isn't worth enough, or you worry that you'll have to pull several all-nighters to get caught up at work. Once you identify the complaint, use curiosity and put on your wide-angle lens. Think about the bigger picture and help the complaint see itself in the scheme of your whole life. Comfort the complaint by reminding it that it is not alone and you are there, too. As you broaden your outlook, how important is the complaint or judgment part you've made against your life or yourself? If you're like most people, the complaint loses its sting when you employ the Practice of Separation, put it in a wider context, and bring compassion and comfort to it.

Making a Gratitude List

Once you put on your wide-angle lens, see yourself totally, with both your imperfections and your strengths, and welcome your limitations as part of your human condition—as aspects of your strength of character rather than personality flaws.

Affirm the blessings that you ordinarily take for granted—those things that would leave your life empty if you didn't have them. Rejoice in your gifts and your uniqueness. Start a list of all the people, places, and things for which you are grateful. Your list can include material items, such as cars, technological conveniences, clothes, jewelry, houses, trips, and so on, as well as loving relationships, children, pets, and colleagues.

Once you've made your list, focus on each item and visualize it as vividly as you can. Be thankful for each item, and feel the gratitude in your heart. Practice this exercise regularly as your feet touch the floor in the morning, on the trip to and from work, or before drifting off to sleep at night. Wanting what you already have and expressing gratitude for it can shift your Confident Self back into the leadership of your life. Your life will become fuller, more satisfying, and more complete, and you will start to see and experience the happiness and abundance that are all around you.

Chapter Six

The Practice of Empowerment

Thinking of yourself as a survivor,
instead of a victim, and accepting
responsibility for your lot

A personality that lives in love and Light, that sees through the eyes of its soul, metaphorically speaking, can see the illusion and simultaneously not be drawn into it. This is an authentically empowered personality.

— *Gary Zukav*

Are You a Survivor or a Victim of Life?

arriet lay in her hospital bed complaining of how sick she was. "There's nothing I can do," she moaned. "My husband has put me here by worrying me so much with his drinking. He's got me so far down that I can't help myself anymore. He's made me think that I'm nothing. If it weren't for him, I wouldn't be in such a bad fix. It's his fault that I had to check into the hospital in the first place!"

It doesn't take a rocket scientist to see that Harriet is a victim of her life conditions. Those of us like Harriet tend to be victim-led in life, or what psychologists call *externalizers*. Simply put, this means they think of themselves as helpless pawns of fate whose lives are determined by external forces outside of themselves. As a result, they externalize their responsibilities, resign themselves to their circumstances, and succumb to fate and chance. They bear little or no responsibility for what happens to them and blame other people and situations for their problems. Externalizers believe that they are blamed for things that are not their fault, that it doesn't pay to try hard because things never turn out right anyway, and that people are mean to them for no reason at all.

This body of research suggests that many people develop this illusion, also known as *learned helplessness*, when they're growing up: no matter what they do, their fate is out of their hands. They are at greater risk of being victimized by life rather than empowered by it, but the good news is that, if you're an *externalizer*, the Practice of Empowerment can help you access your *internalizer* part.

Internalizers (or survivors) are Confident-Led and believe that control of their lives comes from inside themselves. They are masters of their own fate and bear personal responsibility for what happens to them. They believe their own actions determine the positive or negative outcomes in their lives. Internalizers believe that if they do something wrong they can do something to make it right and that they can change what might happen tomorrow by what they do today. Research indicates that those who perceive themselves as being "at cause" instead of "at effect" in their own lives tend to be more optimistic and respond more positively in general to the circumstances they encounter. In other words, they accept their lot and make the best of it, instead of simply enduring it.

Organizational researchers report that survivors are more successful than victims in the workplace. Bellyachers at work, for example, commit career suicide. Offices often become dumping grounds for grousers who struggle with their own internal unhappiness—negative people who lack confidence and feel helpless over their inability to run their personal lives. They don't want to be responsible; they beleaguer problems, expecting someone else to solve them, instead of finding creative solutions. Their chronic whining and complaining infect the work environment and attract other pessimistic workers, forming an "Ain't It Awful" club that poisons morale and sabotages productivity. They don't climb as fast or far up the corporate ladder as confident, harmonious workers who are able to look on the bright side, work as team players, think outside the box, and focus on solutions instead of problems—all forms of survivorship of the work conditions.

When managers decide whether or not to promote a worker, they consider how easy it is to work with the candidate, as well as his or her technical skills. Because whiners and complainers reflect a lack of confidence, colleagues lose confidence in them, too, and managers don't trust them to lead. Self-victimized workers get shut out of top assignments and suffer derailed careers, even if they're competent, because they get stuck in the problems instead of the solutions. They are unable to think optimistically, work as team players, think outside the box, or focus on positive solutions—all because their victim parts eclipse their Confident Selves and they feel victimized by their work conditions.

Katherine, who worked for a well-known computer company, complained to her manager that the new employee with whom she shared an office "made her nervous" because she talked too much. Despite the fact that Katherine had the reputation for being a complainer, her manager complied with Katherine's request to move the office mate to another space. Two weeks later, Katherine whined that her second office mate "made her mad" because she was so messy. Again the manager accommodated her request to move the messy newcomer. After two more episodes of grumbling and moving, it became clear to the manager that the problem originated with Katherine, not any of the four office mates he had shuffled around to accommodate her. Katherine blamed others for her feelings, refused to deal with her problems in a constructive way, and depended upon others to solve her problems for her. The manager, who had been more than willing to accommodate Katherine, unwittingly enabled her victim-led part.

The following are some famous last words of people who lived their lives from their victim parts:

- You ruined my life!
- He makes me so mad.
- I would've done a better job if you hadn't bothered me.
- You're driving me crazy.
- People are always putting me down.
- She's so mean to me.
- I wouldn't drink if you wouldn't nag.
- Your hurrying me caused me to make a mistake.
- It's not my fault.
- I can't help it.
- You got me into this pickle.
- I overeat because of the way my parents treated me.
- It's just the way I am.
- I wouldn't be in this fix if it weren't for you.
- Now look what you've done!
- If you'd just change, everything would be okay.
- This job is ruining my life.

These famous last words reflect how easy it is for our Confident Selves to get hijacked by our victim parts into believing that our problems and solutions are outside of us and succumbing to whatever situation life throws our way. So we blame the people and circumstances for our downfalls and the accompanying pain and suffering. Putting the blame on someone else eclipses confidence and prevents us from seeing that we can take action to change our lives for the better; confidence, thereby, eludes us.

Eleanor Roosevelt observed, "No one can make you feel inferior without your consent." It's true. Nobody can make you doubtful, sick, angry, nervous, or anything else unless you agree to it. Regardless of what happens to us, when we are Confident-Led, we are more conscious of our ability to do something about it. The Practice of Empowerment is a reminder that it isn't the world or the people in it that rob our confidence. It's the victim part that eclipses our power because it doesn't believe in itself.

Many of us become accustomed to thinking of ourselves as downtrodden. Failure, despair, and pessimism become chronic ways of life. Essentially, self-victimization and self-pity become habitual ways of thinking and behaving. This pattern causes victimizers to unwittingly seek out perpetrators. They look for survivors to get them off the responsibility hook, and they are attracted to more confident people who sometimes get accused of being perpetrators of the victim's unhappiness.

The Practice of Empowerment says that life doesn't determine our confidence or lack of it. It's determined by the degree of confidence that leads our lives. We are given life, but we have the power to create our experience of life. If we identify ourselves as helpless victims at the mercy of life's blows, then we will be truly miserable. If we look through the eyes of the Confident Self and see life's illusions, it will empower us to use disadvantages to learn and to create a positive experience out of a negative one. As long as we blame the outside world for our lot in life, we remain victims and disempower ourselves. Once we separate ourselves from our illusions and take responsibility for our thoughts, feelings, and actions, we empower ourselves and improve our lives. The key is to ask not "How is life treating me?" but to ask "How am I treating life?" Even more, it is important to ask "Who is sitting at the head of my internal boardroom table when life is doing its thing? Is it my Confident Self or a victim part of me that needs my understanding and compassion?"

How Are You Treating Life's Cosmic Slaps?

"It was probably the greatest thing that ever happened to me," Jack said, referring to the motorcycle accident that had paralyzed him, because it changed him and helped him grow in ways that otherwise would not have been possible. Jack's ability to see the gains in this huge loss is neither unique nor new.

Actor/comedian Richard Belzer once said, "Cancer is a cosmic slap in the face. You either get discouraged or ennobled by it." In his book *Love, Medicine & Miracles*, the author Bernie Siegel tells the story of a seven-year-old boy whose own words reflected how he saw himself as a survivor of cancer instead of a victim of the disease: "If God wanted me to be a basketball player, he'd have made me seven feet tall. Instead, he gave me cancer so I can be a doctor and help other people."[1]

This child, who had dreamed of a sports career, turned his cancer into an act of love. It empowered him over his disease, and that shows us that we can transform our lives into meaningful life experiences, no matter how horrendous our circumstances.

Everybody is confronted with challenges at one time or another, some small, some seismic. What's important is what we do with them. Turning obstacles into opportunities transforms us from being *passive* recipients of life and allows us to be *active* participants in it. An empowered person (Confident-Led) is learning life's lessons; a victim (parts-led) is enduring life's pain.

In her book *When Things Fall Apart*, Buddhist nun Pema Chodron echoes the theme I present in this book—that sometimes bad news is really good news in disguise:

> Feelings like disappointment, embarrassment, irritation, resentment, anger, jealousy, and fear, instead of being bad news, are actually very clear moments that teach us where it is that we're holding back. They teach us to perk up and lean in when we feel we'd rather collapse and back away. They're like messengers that show us, with terrifying clarity, exactly where we're stuck. This very moment is the perfect teacher, and, lucky for us, it's with us wherever we are.[2]

Many ordinary people have been strengthened by cosmic slaps because they used them to grow. Recovering alcoholics, when telling their "stories," say that when they hit bottom with their drinking, it was the greatest blessing because it catapulted them into a brand-new way of living in sobriety. Clients of mine have claimed that broken intimate relationships—while at first bringing overwhelming grief— often led to other healthier, more meaningful relationships.

Some of the greatest names of our time have surmounted seismic events by finding meaning and gaining strength from them. Christopher Reeve earned the title "Superman," and not just on screen but also in real life. Reeve was slapped with a spinal cord injury and paralysis from the neck down after being thrown from a horse. He inspired millions of people with his courage in the face of his physical disability. Having made a conscious choice to focus on his resources instead of his disability, he dazzled the nation with his empowering, optimistic spirit. He lived a rich and fulfilling life and considered himself to be lucky to have a loving family and close friends. He put his efforts into things he could do, such as acting, directing, and being a spokesperson for spinal cord research.

Survivors transform their suffering and hardships by finding meaning in them. They do this by shifting their views of life's challenges to precious lessons from which they can learn and grow spiritually with the Confident Self in the lead. Rosa Parks made history by refusing to give up her seat on a bus and became a catalyst for erasing discrimination from the law books. Mahatma Gandhi and Martin Luther King used nonviolence in the face of violence to significantly change discrimination practices. Candace Lightner, whose daughter was killed by a drunk driver, started Mothers Against Drunk Driving (MADD) and helped enact stricter legislation against drinking and driving. Born blind and deaf, Helen Keller overcame her disabilities to become one of the great inspirations of our time. Her philosophy of life reflected the meaning she found in her cosmic slap when she said, "Life is either a daring adventure or nothing at all."

For centuries mystics, philosophers, and spiritual leaders have claimed that adversity can enrich our lives if we let it. Life's harsh challenges can strengthen us, bring new meaning to our lives, take us deeper into our own spirituality, and even deepen our closeness to ourselves and others so that we are more connected and more compassionate from the inside out.

Only in recent years have these spiritual and philosophical claims been put to the scientific test. Psychologists interviewed survivors who were slapped with such major trauma as rape, HIV, cancer, intense military combat, natural disaster, severe injury from accidents, death of a child, terminal and chronic illnesses, and job loss. Many of these trauma survivors experienced positive growth through their struggles with the hand life had dealt them. Psychologists noted that these survivors were able to see their lives in a different light and to experience positive growth through their hardships. The survivors said they realized they were stronger than they thought, that they had more emotional closeness and compassion for others, and that they had a deeper appreciation for life, along with a greater openness to spiritual and religious matters.[3] In other words, these survivors found themselves catapulted into a Confident-Led life.

All of us can learn from the scientists, spiritualists, and survivors of cosmic slaps. A veteran of the Iraq War who lost an arm uses his empathy and compassion to counsel other disabled survivors of that war. A person with HIV volunteers time to help raise money for AIDS research and support of other survivors of the disease. A woman, sexually abused as a child, wrote a book about her recovery to help other incest survivors. Perhaps the life struggles and sufferings of others can give us a deeper appreciation for how full and rich our lives truly are. And when life's adversities come your way—as they surely will from time to time—perhaps you can be reminded to look for meaning, strength, and growth in how you face and cope with hardships.

Cosmic slaps are not choices; how you handle them is a choice. You can take the "cosmic taps"—those everyday challenges that are much smaller in scale than devastation— and rework them to your advantage. Finding the gains in your losses will help you lead your life with confidence.

Living the Practice of Empowerment

The Principle of Empowerment puts hardships into a more positive and workable light. It helps you approach problems from the perspective of survivorship so that you can do something about them. It allows you to change the labels you hang on circumstances so that the new tags generate more positive feelings and actions. Practicing the following exercises can help you feel more empowered in your life.

Separating from Your Victim Part

Most of us have a victim part that pops up now and then. This exercise helps you gain distance from that part of you and puts you on the road to empowerment. The next time life hits you hard, instead of blending with the victim part, think of it as a part of you instead of the whole of you. Take a breath and step back from the victim part so that it's not so all engulfing. Once you notice it and can separate from it, try to comfort it. If you're feeling one of the eight "C" words, then befriend the part by getting to know it and establishing a relationship with it on the inside. Sometimes just noticing that you are separate from your victim part helps you remain the "I" in the storm.

The Cosmic Slap Exercise

The Situation: Think of a time when you felt helpless or victimized by a cosmic tap or a seismic slap. Describe the situation objectively without including thoughts or feelings about it.

_____

_____

_____

_____

_____

_____

_____

Your Victimized Reactions: Describe your victimized thoughts, feelings, and actions. If judgment or shame parts pop up, ask them if they'd be willing to step aside just for now, and let curiosity write the descriptions.

_____

_____

_____

_____

_____

_____

_____

Empowerment: Look at your old reactions from the point of view of your Confident Self—in a way that empowers you through a lesson learned or that gives meaning to your helpless thoughts and feelings and that will enable you to think of yourself as a survivor instead of a victim of the life event.

_____

_____

_____

_____

_____

_____

_____

_____

Chapter Seven

The Practice of Harmony

*Surrendering to conditions over which you
have no control and making the best of them*

If a man has nothing to eat, fasting is the most
intelligent thing he can do.

—Herman Hesse

Bending with Life's Curves

Tropical palms are sturdy trees. They survive, not
because they stand rigid and hard against tropical
storms but because they are flexible enough to bend, swing,
and sway with the force of the wind. Few of us have the flu-
idity of these wondrous trees because we become set in our

ways, yet sometimes we are forced to swing and sway when the storms of life overpower us. Otherwise, we would break.

Emily Perl Kingsley wrote about such an unwelcome life event in her story of having a son with Down syndrome:

> I am often asked to describe the experience of raising a child with a disability—to try to help people who have not shared that unique experience to understand it, to imagine how it would feel. It's like this. . . .
>
> When you're going to have a baby, it's like planning a fabulous vacation trip to Italy. You buy a bunch of guidebooks and make your wonderful plans. The Coliseum. Michelangelo's *David*. The gondolas in Venice. You may even learn some handy phrases in Italian. It's all very exciting.
>
> After months of eager anticipation, the day finally arrives. You pack your bags and off you go. Several hours later the plane lands. The stewardess comes in and says, "Welcome to Holland."
>
> "Holland?" you say. "What do you mean, Holland? I signed up for Italy. I'm supposed to be in Italy. All my life I've dreamed of going to Italy."
>
> But there's been a change in the flight plan. They've landed in Holland and there you must stay.
>
> The important thing is that they haven't taken you to a horrible, disgusting, filthy place, full of pestilence, famine, and disease. It's just a different place.
>
> So you must go out and buy new guidebooks. And you must learn a whole new language. And you will meet a whole new group of people you would never have met.

It's just a different place. It's slower-paced than Italy, less flashy than Italy. But after you've been there for a while and you catch your breath, you look around and you begin to notice that Holland has windmills, Holland has tulips. Holland even has Rembrandts.

But everyone you know is busy coming and going from Italy, and they're all bragging about what a wonderful time they had there. And for the rest of your life, you will say, "Yes, that's where I was supposed to go. That's what I had planned."

And the pain of that will never, ever, ever, ever go away . . . because the loss of that dream is a very, very significant loss.

But . . . if you spend your life mourning the fact that you didn't get to Italy, you may never be free to enjoy the very special, the very lovely things about Holland.[1]

When we've planned to be in Italy, most of us at some point will find ourselves in Holland, because life always throws us one of its curveballs. This curveball can come as an unexpected death of a loved one, a broken marriage, a sudden loss of a job, a devastating illness, damage to our home from a natural disaster, knowledge that a child is gay or lesbian—and much more.

The key is to allow our Confident Self to lead on this unexpected journey so that we can adjust to wherever we end up. In a Barbara Walters interview, Elizabeth Taylor said she laughed when doctors told her she had a brain tumor. Walters gasped. But Taylor wisely replied, "What else are you going to do?"

Spiritualist Anthony de Mello has said it is our overattachment to the outcomes in life that doom us to a life of frustration, anxiety, worry, insecurity, suspense, and tension:

> Once your attachment had you in its grip, you began to strive might and main, every waking minute of your life, to rearrange the world around you so that you could attain and maintain the objects of your attachment. This is an exhausting task that leaves you little energy for the business of living and enjoying life fully. It is also an impossible task in an ever-changing world that you simply are not able to control.[2]

We use a lot of energy getting upset over things we cannot control, instead of accepting and making the best of them. When life throws us a curve, it is an opportunity to bend. Instead of resisting unwelcome changes (which ego parts want to help us do to help us survive), the Confident-Led life helps us face them and find meaning and purpose and learn from them, no matter how painful they are.

Therapists have a saying: "What we resist persists." A more down-home expression I learned in the South is "When treed by a bear, enjoy the view." Ask yourself if you have resisted an unwelcome event in your life over which you have no control. Then decide what you can do to bend with the situation. Confucius said, "The grass must bend when the wind blows over it." You can resist and break, or you can bend like grass. The Practice of Harmony—the ability to fully surrender to situations over which you have no control and make the best of them—is the hallmark of the Confident-Led Life.

Straitjacketed Lives

An ancient tale about Nasrudin illustrates how even today some of us straitjacket our lives when we go against the grain of the Practice of Harmony:

Nasrudin longed for the love of a beautiful woman in his village whom he'd seen but who'd never paid him any attention. Nasrudin heard about a love potion in a faraway land that would make any woman of your dreams fall in love with you.

He took the trip, purchased the potion, and slipped it into the woman's drink as she ate lunch in a local restaurant. The woman fell instantly and completely head over heels in love with Nasrudin, and they soon married. But Nasrudin was miserable in the marriage. He couldn't eat or sleep, and his work fell by the wayside.

Eventually, he couldn't even bring himself to touch his bride. He spent every waking hour agonizing over a question to which he'd never get an answer: "Would she love me if it were not for the love potion?" Nasrudin learned that, no matter how much you love someone, their love cannot be commanded.

When ego parts run our lives, they make things fit with what they think we want or need instead of fitting into the scheme of things beyond our control. The need for control spills over into controlling other people and situations. But no matter how well intended they are or how hard they try, the ego parts cannot make the world and the people in it function the way they want.

When ego parts are in charge and things don't go our way, instead of making the best of them, we blow up at the conditions. We throw a fit when the football game or parade is rained or snowed out. We shake our fists at the heavens because we're behind and twenty-four hours in the day are not enough. We beat the steering wheel in traffic jams. We go ballistic when the computer crashes. We freak out over fender benders and airline flight delays. And we steamroll our agendas over people at work or church instead of listening to their ideas. We stonewall (instead of tolerate) people who have beliefs, opinions, or lifestyles different from ours. We sigh and stomp our feet in long slow-moving lines. We become annoyed with people who are late, forget appointments, bake bread differently, move slower, or take different routes to the mall. It's as if we're trying to fit a square peg into a round hole or a size-nine foot into a size-seven shoe.

Life can feel like a battleground, like one perpetual struggle after another. We cannot persuade the boss to see our point of view; we cannot scrounge enough money to purchase the new car; we cannot sway the opinions of colleagues to reach a decision at work; we cannot convince our partner, spouse, or roommate that our decision about the household makes the most sense.

We may find ourselves constantly arguing with family members or harshly disagreeing with coworkers. Everybody, it seems, is against us. After a while we must face the facts. If we are constantly squabbling with others, who is the common denominator? Even when we know in our hearts that there are many ways to skin a cat, that our actions are not working, or that a colleague has a better strategy, our ego parts refuse to concede.

When we feel as if we're constantly battling and losing, we can step back and look at what's going on inside and outside of us. We can consider if an *oppositional part* has drawn battle lines, trying to force its will by refusing to hear other points of view, or if *argumentative, aggressive, overbearing, arrogant,* and *self-indulgent parts* are ready to strike with combative strategies. Perhaps we create war within ourselves and don't even know it. Keep in mind that all these ego parts are working diligently to protect and provide us with the best life has to offer, and their intentions are admirable, despite the outcomes. So wink at the parts trying to help you out, and see if they'd be willing to collaborate with your Confident Self.

Mind-sets, hardheadedness, negative attitudes, fear of change, inflexibility, stinginess, impatience, anger, resentment, hesitation, withholding feelings, rigidity, whining, chronic complaining, and *pessimism* are all straitjacketed parts that can keep us stuck in disharmony. Each part has its own agenda and advocates for its own way to solve life's problems. These ego parts just don't see the bigger picture, whereas our leader, the Confident Self, sees through a wide-angle lens and leads from that perspective.

Forcing, Resisting, and Clinging

Many great teachings and spiritual practices state that peace of mind comes from going with the flow instead of imposing our will by forcing, resisting, and clinging, which create disharmony in our lives. *Forcing* is an *offensive reaction* in which the ego manipulates, controls, and imposes its will on other people and situations. *Resisting* is a *defensive reaction* in which the ego blocks the truth about other people or refuses to accept life circumstances through denial or blocking in some way. *Clinging* is an *avoidance reaction* in which the ego clutches the familiar and avoids change or the unknown in favor of habit and routine. In his book *The Five Things We Cannot Change,* David Richo says freeing ourselves from the grip of the ego is not a loss but an emancipation.[3]

Living with confidence involves taking a personal inventory and asking what we may have been forcing, resisting, or clinging to that merits letting go. For example, do you push for Chinese food when out with friends who prefer Mexican? Do you pressure loved ones to live their lives to suit you? Do you boss colleagues with your way of doing things when you could be more of a team player? Do you resist other points of view instead of stretching your mind and heart to see their side of the story? Do you cling to your youth instead of facing your age and aging gracefully? Do you hold on to relationships that are over instead of moving on to a healthier life? Do you stick with stale ruts and routines, or do you think outside the box and try new things?

After you have identified a pattern in your life, ask yourself what you can do differently that would put you more in harmony with your life. You need rules, routines, and schedules to keep your life orderly, but when your ego clings too tightly to them (e.g., you live a clockwork life, dotting every *i* and crossing every *t*, unyielding to flexible schedules and rules), it can create disharmony. You can also create disharmony by flying by the seat of your pants without organization or boundaries. Some people fear grounding themselves with routines or commitments because they don't want to be tied down or held back and because they're afraid they'll miss the moment if they organize and plan, and they often accomplish little.

Whether you live your life by the book or fly by the seat of your pants, the rigidity of both extremes limits the potential in your life. Frequenting the same restaurants, holding the same job, following the same daily routines, staying in the same close-knit circle of friends, holding on to the same ruts and routes might feel familiar and comfortable, but these activities block confidence. Some people cling to old ways because they are familiar and predictable, and there's always the hope that maybe this time things will be better. To others, the unfamiliarity of new and different ways and ideas might feel threatening to ego parts whose motives are to keep them safe at all costs. Ego parts often resist the Confident Self even though their relaxing would allow the Confident Self to make the changes that are needed.

Stick Your Neck Out

There is a difference in giving up (helplessness led by an ego part) and surrendering (powerlessness led by the Confident Self). Helplessness is when you shrug your shoulders and forgo the courage to change the things you can. Powerlessness is when you know what you can and cannot change and surrender to situations beyond your control. This action actually empowers you because it puts you in the most powerful position you can be in: that of a survivor instead of a victim. Leading a confident life is a tightwire walk between knowing when to surrender to situations and when to stick your neck out. Playing it safe can be just as disharmonious as pushing against a river's flow.

Antoine de Saint Exupery said, "We are afraid to let go of our petty reality in order to grasp at a great shadow." Another ancient tale about Nasrudin, who lost his house key on the way home one night, illustrates how some have *scared parts* that are afraid for us to stick out our necks:

> Nasrudin was on all fours under the streetlamp, searching frantically for his house key, when a stranger happened by and asked him what he was looking for. Nasrudin told him he had lost his house key. The stranger, being a kind man, got down on his hands and knees and helped look for it.
>
> After hours of searching with no success, the stranger asked, "Are you sure you dropped the key in this spot?"
>
> Nasrudin said, "Oh, no! I dropped it way over there in that dark alley."

Frustrated and angry, the stranger lost his temper. "Then why are you looking for it here?"

"Because the light's better here under the streetlamp," Nasrudin replied.

Many of us, like Nasrudin, spend our lives playing it safe, searching in familiar places for the key to a Confident Life. We resist exploring new areas that appear unfamiliar or threatening, even when they might lead to illumination. This results in little success at finding confidence because a scared part keeps us under the safety of the lamppost.

Although the ego prefers sameness and resists change, change is the one thing we can count on. Clinging to the familiar and comfortable puts you at odds with the natural flow of life. No matter how hard you clutch old ways, change will drag you kicking and screaming into doing things differently. The solutions are often in the shadows. Sometimes it takes venturing into the darkness where we've never been—getting acquainted with the parts holding us back, understanding their concerns, and developing compassion for them. These internal actions can bring us into the light with confidence in the lead. As a result, our external lives automatically start to feel more harmonious.

A colleague said she doesn't like to do anything at which she cannot succeed. She said it gives her a feeling of satisfaction to do things perfectly. At work she avoids certain responsibilities and challenges for fear of not doing them well. She won't go white-water rafting or swimming because she'd feel foolish learning how.

"I cannot swim," she told me, "because as an adult it's embarrassing to take swimming lessons. The only way I could do it is if they would clear the pool so nobody could witness me being inept as an adult in something that almost everybody else knows how to do."

Are you the type of person who only accepts challenges in which you can shine right from the start? Do you avoid situations that require you to learn from your mistakes? If so, your avoidance of failure can turn into the avoidance of success because success is built on failing. My colleague felt she hadn't achieved what she'd hoped for in her intimate and professional lives because she hadn't taken the necessary risks for success. That's because she was led internally by *avoidant and perfectionistic ego parts*, which were protecting her deeper fear of failure, which originated in her childhood.

The road to the Confident Life is paved with a series of fears and failures. Once you accept them as essential stepping-stones to confidence and take the risk anyway, you give yourself permission to make the mistakes necessary to get where you want to go. You can start by identifying a fear that has crippled you or prevented you from succeeding. It can be as straightforward as learning to swim or balancing your checkbook or as considerable as speaking your mind before a group of peers, confronting a colleague over a wrongdoing, or launching a new business venture. Find just one place in your life where you can stick your neck out. As you face and comfort your fear (instead of ignoring or plowing over it), you'll unearth greater confidence and find yourself one lap closer to the life you've been wanting.

You can use this approach to eliminate the boredom and roadblocks to confidence that sameness creates. Welcome opposing views, knowing that everyone's way of thinking is different from yours but valid nonetheless. Use your creativity to get out of ruts and change your daily routines, even if it's as simple as taking a different route home from work. If you've been unsuccessful at relationships, take a different approach. Choose just one thing to do differently, no matter how trivial, that you've never done before. If you feel an inner resistance, check in with the part using curiosity, and see what concerns might be there. Let the resistance feel your compassion and confidence. Then stand back and watch your life bloom.

The Power of Surrender

Accepting conditions that are beyond your control and surrendering to them can bring you instant calm because you can't do anything about them anyway. Circumstances change once we accept them *exactly* as they are, no matter how difficult, frustrating, and painful. When we *accept* each uncontrollable situation exactly as it is — instead of trying to make it the way we want it to be — we surrender, making ourselves harmonious with it and, therefore, surmounting it. As a result, our lives run more smoothly.

The Twelve Steps of Alcoholics Anonymous, which embody the Practice of Harmony, have saved millions of lives from the devastation of substance abuse, eating disorders, gambling, sex addiction, and workaholism. The Serenity Prayer, the bedrock of these recovery programs, helps ego parts to relax and the calm, Confident Self to emerge: "God grant me the serenity to accept the things I cannot change, the courage to change the things I can, and the wisdom to know the difference." The Practice of Harmony has brought hope, courage, and inner peace to millions of people who learn to accept and surrender, to let go and let God.

The Practice of Harmony can bring all of us more confident lives, regardless of whether or not we are in a recovery program. The more we study the natural order of things and go with it, rather than resist it, the more we become harmonious with the world and find peace of mind. The Chinese philosopher Lao Tzu said, "Simply notice the natural order of things. Work with it rather than against it. For to try to change what is, only sets up resistance."

We live on a planet that is perfectly planned. Our world is orderly and predictable because it is governed by laws that have operated from the beginning of time. The tides know how to move the oceans. Gravity knows how to hold things down. The planets know how to maintain their alignment in relation to the sun. Earth knows how to spin on its axis. Perfect harmony prevails.

Physicists agree that the universe operates in an orderly, explainable fashion rather than randomly and haphazardly. Scientists believe that the physical world unfolds according to the law of cause and effect, with one event causing another, which causes another, and so on. Life is not tailored to our specifications, and it does not bend to fit our lifestyles. Henry Miller once said, "The world is *not* to be put in order, the world *is* order incarnate."

With that in mind, you can surmount hardships by surrendering to them—accepting them without complaints or resistance, knowing they are happening in an orderly, explainable fashion—and taking positive action wherever you can. These actions take courage, and the wisdom of Rainer Maria Rilke, one of the greatest twentieth-century poets, offers comfort—"Let everything happen to you: beauty and terror. Just keep going. No feeling is final."

Surrendering to the natural flow gives us more power than pushing against the natural laws of nature. Martial arts instructors teach that if an aggressor pushes you, your position is strengthened when you surrender to their energy by pulling them, instead of pushing back (which is a form of resistance). If an aggressor pulls you, pushing instead of pulling away (which is another form of resistance) overpowers the attacker. Lamaze childbirth has been shown to be a smoother, less complicated form of childbirth than more conventional methods because expectant parents breathe with natural labor contractions, instead of tightening up and working against them. When your company is moving in one direction that goes against your grain and you can do nothing to stop it, your best position is to adapt. If the direction goes against your ethics, values, or personal goals, you might need to find another job that is more harmonious. If you're in an unhealthy relationship and you've changed all the things you can, but it still doesn't feel right for you, it may be time to take yourself out of the unhealthy relationship.

Empathy Neutralizes Disharmony

Imagine having dinner with someone special in an expensive restaurant. You've looked forward to a quiet evening of candlelight, soft music, and intimate conversation. Your server, however, is invasive, impatient, and short tempered. How would you feel? What would you do? Most people would get annoyed or angry and perhaps tell her off.

Now imagine that a friend who's eating at the restaurant and knows the server comes over to inform you that the server's son was killed in a car wreck but she had to work anyway because she's a single mom with a meager income. How would you feel? Most people would feel sad, sorry, or empathetic. What happened? How can your emotions switch from anger one second to compassion the next? The server didn't change. She is continuing the same behaviors, but something inside you changed. The way you were looking at the situation changed because you have a bigger context in which to see this woman. This insight from the Confident Self, instead of a part, might even lead you to leave a large tip, despite the lousy service.

Empathy neutralizes the disharmonious parts of us. The ability to put yourself in someone else's shoes and see their point of view is a powerful technique that pays off. By deliberately putting yourself in someone else's place and feeling what it's like to be them, you increase your understanding and sensitivity. It liberates you from narrow and negative viewpoints and helps you be less judgmental. Using this technique can help you respond to situations in more confident ways, experiencing difficult people and situations with less frustration and more peace of mind.

Suppose you buy a defective iPod and you call the store to complain. If the salesperson is unsympathetic and uncooperative, you'd probably get madder (a part of you would get triggered). If she apologizes for your inconvenience and says something like "I know that must have been frustrating for you!" and promises to make the purchase right, you'd feel your anger subside. That's because the salesperson joined you in your frustration (surrendering to your point of view), thereby diffusing your anger.

Empathy—in our jobs, marriages, or friendships—is a form of surrender because we suspend our point of view and walk in the other person's shoes for a while. This form of surrender is another example of your confidence leading the way, which can have huge payoffs in personal and professional relationships.

You can use this technique with friends and loved ones to help settle disputes or to help you stay calm when someone else is exploding. Suppose you've had an enjoyable day of serenity and relaxation when all of a sudden your spouse (or partner) comes bounding through the house, cursing and slamming doors. Most likely you would resent the fact that he or she is raining on your parade. You might even start slamming things and cursing yourself. However, if you take the time to consider with curiosity what lies below the surface of your partner's upset, you're more likely to have clarity about the cause of the huff, and that will neutralize your anger and help you respond with compassion. Suppose, for example, your loved one was fired, was in a car wreck, or was just diagnosed with a terminal illness. Whatever the root cause, taking time to discover it before you react can help you stay in your Confident Self and become more the kind of person you want to be.

Now you might be thinking, *But why should I be empathetic to someone who's blasting me—loved one or stranger? That just doesn't make sense!* First, using empathy rather than anger as a first response can make you a more loving, kind, and compassionate person. And if that's not reason enough, empathy allows you to maintain control over a situation, keeping your cool intact. It enables you to see the full situation from more than just your vantage point (a wide-angle lens versus a zoom lens) and to respond in a way that facilitates clear communication. In professional situations, taking the higher ground of understanding with a client or coworker with a gripe actually can give you the upper hand and can diffuse the situation, allowing you to be more effective.

Living the Practice of Harmony

The way to live the Practice of Harmony is to see if you can develop a relationship with your control part by seeing if it would be willing to relax and work with your Confident Self, instead of running roughshod over your lead. We need our control part to function efficiently, but at times we don't need it to push so hard, especially in situations that are beyond our control, or when we need to step out from between other people and their problems, trusting them to find their own solutions, or when we need to stop getting mad at things beyond our control, to start accepting them and molding our lives to fit within them.

Letting-Go Exercise

Are you a forcer, resister, or clinger? Think of as many things as you can that you force, resist, or cling to in your life. It could be forcing your point of view on someone who has his or her own perspective. Or it could be resisting a life change—either an inner change or a situational change. It could be refusing to accept a part of you that you've ignored or someone's behavior that is beyond your control. Or it could be unwillingness to try something new—a new relationship, a new experience, or a new way of doing something.

In the exercise below, list each aspect of your life you are forcing, resisting, or clinging to in the left column. In the right column, list what you can do to accept and surrender to this part of your life.

THE LETTING-GO EXERCISE

I am forcing . . .   I can accept and surrender

_____

to this part of my life.

I am resisting . . .   I can accept and surrender

_____

to this part of my life.

I am clinging to . . .   I can accept and surrender

_____

to this part of my life.

In your daily life, when you find yourself forcing, resisting, or clinging to things or people over which you have no control, step back from the situation. Look objectively at what's going on. See if your ego can relax and let go so that you can take other courses of action that bring more harmony to your life.

The following meditations can help you let go and live more harmoniously. You can say them silently to yourself when you're having difficulty with giving up control.

FORCING: *I admit that I am powerless over controlling my world and that when I force things, my life becomes unmanageable. I will try to surrender to the things I cannot control and turn my will and my life over to life's natural order.*

RESISTING: *Today I will catch myself when I start to resist that which I cannot control. I will check in with my resistance in an effort to understand its concerns and ask it to relax so that I can open myself to the lessons that life offers me and make the best out of whatever comes my way.*

CLINGING: *Today I practice hands off and follow the grand harmony of the universe. Instead of clinging to old ways, unhealthy habits, and people who disrespect me, I try to understand what purpose the clinging serves and to see if it can be more open to change. I am learning the rules of life and how fitting into them can foster my faith and help me live with confidence.*

Walk a Mile in Someone's Shoes

Think of someone who has done something to upset you—a personal friend, love interest, or coworker—with whom you can empathize right now. Temporarily surrender your point of view (you don't have to give it up for good) and look at the situation from the other person's standpoint. Try to imagine walking around inside that person's body and experiencing the upsetting event in their skin, through their eyes, and with their heart. Without getting into who's right and who's wrong, ask yourself if there is any aspect of the other person's perspective that you can validate (without giving up your point of view). If so, then notice if your upset feelings dissipate somewhat.

Chapter Eight

The Practice of
the Unmade Mind

*Keeping your mind unmade,
instead of made up, in new situations*

If your only tool is a hammer, everything you see
will be a nail.

—Abraham Maslow

Murphy's Law? Be Careful
How You Connect the Dots

A funny thing happened to me while I waited for a bus
at the Honolulu zoo. A small red sports car was stalled
in the middle of the street, and a police officer was talking to

the driver. The stalled car caused a traffic jam, and angry passengers leaned on their horns. A passerby walked over to check out the disruption, smirked, and admonished the officer for throwing his weight around and causing the traffic jam. The angry woman, having made up a scenario about what happened, carried a misperception of that event with her forever. She stormed off, gesturing wildly and loudly, protesting, "If he wants to give her a ticket, why doesn't he pull her over to the side, instead of tying up traffic?"

The officer raised the hood of the car, sat in the driver's seat, and tried unsuccessfully to start the engine. When we have our minds made up, we see illusions of what we think happened and who we think people are instead of the objective truth about them.

The lightbulb burns out in the bathroom, bedroom, and kitchen—all at the same time. The car has a flat tire on the way to the office, where you discover a shortage of paper clips. Your cable TV is on the blink. Little things can make your life feel like it's falling apart. So you scream, you rant, and you rave.

"Murphy's Law!" you exclaim. "If something can go wrong in my life, it certainly will." But is it Murphy's Law or your ego personalizing random, everyday irritations?

Let me explain why there is no science behind Murphy's Law, which is really just a close-minded ego part that expects the worst in your life. You drop a piece of buttered toast, and it always falls butter side down. Just your bad luck, you say? Not according to science. Research scientist Robert A. Matthews at Aston University in Birmingham, England, put this question to the test. Matthews found that buttered toast almost always falls buttered side down because of the law of physics. The rate of spin of falling buttered toast is too slow to allow it to make a complete revolution and come face up again before it hits the floor. Not Murphy's Law at all, he concludes.

Another example: You seem to choose the slowest-moving line at the grocery store. Murphy's Law, you contend? Not according to Matthews. The truth is that all lines move more or less at the same speed. Each will have its own delays that occur randomly: such as changing cash register tape or a customer who forgets a grocery item. Suppose there are three lines, and you pick one. According to the law of averages, two-thirds of the time either the line to your left or the one to your right will beat yours.

Those lightbulbs that all burn out at once were most likely installed at the same time and have a similar life expectancy. Chances are that the situations your ego writes off to negative things happening to you have a scientific basis and have nothing to do with how you're connecting the dots. So when you find yourself overreacting to things not going your way or operating according to plan, remind your triggered part that you are experiencing life's random events. The universe isn't against you, and you're not jinxed. You are simply experiencing the random laws of nature.

Over the course of my twenty years as a psychotherapist, I have treated people who claim that something must be wrong with them because they cannot find the person of their dreams. Invariably, I find that these interesting, great-looking folks have an unconscious ego part that has already decided that there is no one for them (Murphy's Law). Still, they go on the date, their inner protective parts alerted, which might cause them to play their cards close to their chests, make snap judgments, or allow negative qualities to overshadow positive ones. They might come across as uptight, fumbling, or overly apologetic. I try to help them see that a protective part of them has already decided the outcome, and this ego part unwittingly acts in ways that confirm what it already believes. In other words, nothing is wrong with them (not Murphy's Law, after all), but it's the science of what they're doing that sabotages their success at dating.

Suppose you meet someone new, and after the first date they don't call again. Your conclusion? *I guess I'm not very interesting* or *I'm not attractive enough.* A month later you find out that your date was sick in bed with the flu for a week, and not calling had nothing whatsoever to do with you. You spent all that time agonizing *What's wrong with me?* Your mind (i.e., judgment part) was already made up about the date before you had the hard facts, and it blamed you unjustly without evidence. The anti-dote to this mind reading—transferring illusions from previous experience onto new situations, instead of seeing situations for what they are—lies in the Practice of the Unmade Mind.

The Self-Fulfilling Prophecy

You, like almost everybody, probably have expectations of how situations will play out before they happen. Usually when you expect a situation to be a certain way, that's the way it turns out, because an ego-led part thinks and behaves in ways that make your thoughts come true. This part is called the *self-fulfilling prophecy.*

When you carry expectations around and superimpose them in the present, it prevents you from seeing the present clearly as it really is. Your expectations create a mind-set of how events will unfold and people will behave before they do, and you enter situations with your mind already made up about the outcome. Often, when you expect a situation to be bad, it turns out that way, because you think and behave—unconsciously—to make it fit your expectations.

Made-up minds cause you to miss opportunities to learn and love. Expectations, already planted in your mind, influence how you view and treat colleagues, friends, and loved ones and how you interpret conversations. Although it is important to learn from experience, it's also important to be aware when preconceptions (old ego parts) eclipse your Confident Self and cloud new experiences. This is the basis for prejudice, hatred, and wars.

Metaphysicians have long held that our thoughts and expectations create our realities. In his book *The Cosmic*

Power Within You, Joseph Murphy explains this process from
a metaphysical viewpoint:

> Whatever your conscious reasoning mind accepts as true engen-
> ders a corresponding reaction from your subconscious mind which
> is one with Infinite Intelligence within you. Your subconscious
> mind works through the creative law which responds to the nature
> of your thought, bringing about conditions, experiences and events
> in the image and likeness of your habitual thought patterns.[1]

Research scientists have conducted many studies proving
that we see what we expect to see. In one study, a group of
adults was asked to observe a nine-month-old baby playing
with a jack-in-the-box. The scientists told one half of the
observers that the infant was a boy and told the other half
that the infant was a girl. Asked to describe the infant's reactions when the jack popped out of the box, the observers who
thought the baby was a girl said she was "fearful." And those
who thought the baby was a boy described him as "angry."
The point of the study? To demonstrate that when we carry
two different beliefs into the same situation, we expect, look
for, and see two different things because the ego-led mind is
guided by our two different sets of expectations.

The most famous experiment on self-fulfilling prophecies
dealt with the expectations that schoolteachers had for their
pupils' achievement. Teachers were told that a handful of
their students had been identified as intellectual "late

bloomers." The teachers were told that these kids were expected to show unusually big achievement gains during the upcoming school year.

The truth of the matter was that the children identified as exceptionally intelligent had, in fact, been randomly selected and placed in the classroom. Thus, there was no reason, other than the teachers' mind-sets, to expect high gains in achievement. Test results at the end of the school year showed that the children indeed had higher leaps in performance—gains that were attributed to teacher expectations, which caused the teachers to treat the students differently and the children to respond in kind with higher-level performances.[2]

These findings apply not just to how we treat children but also to the way we all approach life in general. You can create positive reactions to situations in the same way that you create negative ones—by having positive thoughts and behaving in ways that make them come true. Being open to new experiences and trying not to have your mind made up can actually work in your favor.

A basic premise of Buddhism is to treat your mind like a bed that you keep unmade instead of made up—the beginner's mind. If the ego is already made up and already has things figured out (which is one of the ways the ego protects us), then clarity in the present can be compromised. You will not be able to learn from new experiences or receive insights from them.

The story of the farmer and the stranger is a good illustration of how this practice works:

Once there was a farmer working in the field, when down the road came a stranger. "I've been thinking of moving," said the stranger, "and I wonder what kind of people live around here." "Well," replied the farmer, "what kind of people live where you come from?" "Not very good," answered the stranger. "They're selfish and mean and not at all friendly. I'll be glad to leave them behind!"

"Well," said the farmer, "I expect you'll find the same sort of people around here . . . selfish and mean and not at all friendly. You probably won't like it here."

The stranger went on. Shortly afterward, another stranger came along the same road.

"I've been thinking of moving," said the stranger, "and I wonder what kind of people live around here."

"Well," replied the farmer, "what kind of people live where you come from?"

"Oh, wonderful people!" answered the stranger. "They're generous and kind and very friendly. I'll really be sorry to leave them."

"Well," said the farmer, "I expect you'll find the same sort of people around here . . . generous and kind and very friendly. I'm sure you'll like it here."

The point of this tale is that expectations can prevent us from leading confident lives. We expect the worst from situations that haven't happened yet. We expect too much of ourselves and others—feeling perpetually let down. We expect others to provide our emotional security. We expect ourselves to perform better and faster. We expect life to be problem free. These types of expectations leave us stressed out and resentful.

Expectations Are Premeditated Resentments

A man I know reluctantly invited his mother for a visit. Although he loved her, he had difficulty being around her because she was negative and grumpy (i.e., he resented her). Two days before her visit he had butterflies in his stomach, thinking of the arguments they would have and how upset she would make him. The man had already created the outcome of the weekend visit. Sure enough, all his negative images came true.

Another example: Suppose you're going for a job interview and a friend tells you that the interviewer is friendly, kind, and easy to talk to. No doubt you will go into the interview with an ease and calm that will be picked up by the employer, which will give him a positive impression of you. His positive impression, in turn, will indicate to you through his smiles and positive comments that he is impressed with you. This feedback will cause you to continue to present yourself in a self-confident way that will probably get you the job.

In contrast, suppose your friend tells you that the same man is a perfectionistic grouch. He is very hard to please, and you will never be able to do anything right in his view. Unless you are applying the Practice of the Unmade Mind, you would probably begin the job interview feeling apprehensive. Your shaken confidence may cause you to forget to smile, to appear nervous or perhaps even incompetent. The employer might sense your discomfort and form an impression of you as edgy, perhaps weak, or unable to function under pressure. (Remember, employers, too, are operating from their own expectations.) Your discomfort might even make the employer feel uncomfortable, causing him to develop a negative impression of you. You begin to sense that displeasure when he develops a cold, detached demeanor in response to your seriousness and discomfort.

The same practice operates in intimate relationships when our minds are already made up. I had a patient named Jake who came to counseling because he was obsessed with the unfounded belief that his wife was going to cheat on him. Jake's fear part so controlled him that he monitored his wife's every move. At parties he wouldn't let her out of his sight. Jake followed her to get drinks and even to the restroom, where he waited outside for her. He sent her flowers and cards every day and told her he loved her every hour on the hour. If you were Jake's wife, imagine how nerve-racking it would have been to have someone hovering over you and anticipating your every move. It was a maddening experience for her to the point that she contemplated leaving the marriage.

The paradox is that those of us who have a fear of abandonment often create it by holding on too tightly to the ones we love and strangling the life out of the relationship. After a while, loved ones can't take the stress of confinement and they leave, confirming the worst nightmare of the worrier. Our expectations have self-fulfilling effects so that our experiences of life become whatever we expect them to be. In other words, we see what we expect to see and create positive or negative situations when we expect to see them.

Fear and love are opposites. It's impossible to fully love someone if you're constantly afraid of losing them. The paradox is that when a relationship is fear led, you will end up creating the very thing that you were afraid would happen. So what do you do about the fear of abandonment? Start with finding out where your fear comes from. The answers almost always lie in the past. Jake, for example, told me of the time as an excited nine-year-old he rushed home to share his good grades with his mother. As he barged through her bedroom door, his confused eyes saw her in bed with their preacher. She beat and scolded him for intruding into her bedroom. Jake's enthusiasm was squashed, his trust in close loved ones permanently fractured. As a young adult, every woman he loved before meeting his wife cheated on him. Jake's expectation that you cannot trust women was a belief he imposed on his wife, who was a virgin when he met her and who had never even thought about cheating on him.

I suggested to him that it wasn't reasonable to blame his wife for what his mother and girlfriends had done in his youth. To save his marriage, I helped him connect with the expectation part that expected his wife to cheat on him. The expectation part was trying to help him keep his wife from cheating so he wouldn't be hurt again, but it was unwittingly creating the opposite effect. Eventually, Jake was able to separate compassionately from the expectation part of him and to connect more with his Confident Self. This practice allowed him to see his wife differently and to change his behavior accordingly—a freedom that helped him relax in the marriage and made her want to be closer to him instead of push him away.

A Confident Relationship is built on freedom, not domination. Strong relationships are based on trust and freedom; weak relationships are based on fear, which leads to imposed authority and domination. If you have nagging thoughts that *He's going to leave me* or *She's going to find someone else*, chances are that a past experience is causing those expectations—an old experience that has nothing to do with your present one. The part of you that is wounded from the old hurt could be collecting evidence based on its unfounded fears and burdening your current relationship. These unfounded fears can damage your intimacy, putting distance between you and your beloved. When you separate yourself from the wounded part and develop a comforting relationship with it, you can stop acting from it and see your loved ones for who they really are.

Waiting for the Ax to Fall

Kimberly had great difficulty with weekends and holidays when she had too much free time. Waking up on a morning with nothing to do left her with a feeling of foreboding. She felt fidgety during those idle hours, that if she let her guard down she'd surely be hit by all the bad things she worried about in her quiet hours. So she coped with worry by staying on guard for the unexpected, even when everything was okay. She packed her weekends full and overscheduled her life so that it would feel more predictable, so she'd know exactly what would happen next and how to prepare for it. Although staying busy seemed to alleviate worry, it robbed her of flexibility, spontaneity, relaxing moments, play, and just plain enjoyment of the present.

Do you continue to be afraid for reasons long past? Does your body still carry the reflex of these old fears—a flip-flop in the stomach, a tightness in the shoulders, a "What if" in the brain? *What if I don't get the promotion? What if they don't like me?*

I don't have to tell you how these intrusive thoughts can disrupt a Confident Life that keeps you stuck in the past and future—a bleak future that your mind has made up—causing you to miss the present altogether. Although it has honorable intentions, *worry* can feel like one of those cruel ghosts of the made-up mind, haunting you day and night, recycling the past through the present. Will I make my quota? Will my job be here next year? Am I still attractive? Will my marriage last?

Worry (an ego part) goes ahead of you like a scouting party, warning of challenging situations that you will soon be facing. On the inside, though, it can feel like a stalker, lurking over your shoulder when you are having a stressful day at work or struggling with intimate relationships. Like all protective ego parts, though, worry is a constant reminder that you don't have forever to complete your tasks on Earth. When you are worry-led, instead of Confident-Led, the anchor of worry can weigh you down and bring you to your knees as you cart around all your problems from the past, from the present, and those that you expect to have in the future. When worry turns "What ifs" over and over in your mind, they expand, and your thoughts about them become distorted to the point that you're dealing with a magnification of the problem — not the problem itself.

Sometimes the biggest worries occur when everything is going well, and you tell yourself that things are just too good to be true. Instead of embracing the calm, your mind braces for the worst. When worry pirates your life during both calm *and* troubled times, you have a worry-filled life 24/7. Living this way robs you of the happy, confident times to which you're entitled.

Although it doesn't mean to, worry weakens you physically, keeping you in the fight-or-flight mode — a state of emergency in which your body secretes adrenaline, creating wear and tear on your body, as if you are actually going through the dreaded experience. The consequences are emotional exhaustion, burnout, and physical ailments.

Are you waiting for the ax to fall or worrying that something bad might happen, even though there's no good reason for it? If so, start with curiosity to see if you can get more clarity about this active part of you. Remind yourself that worry is only a premeditated thought searching for evidence, a synapse firing in your brain. As you separate from the part, see if you can understand where it came from and why it's so active. In its own way, it's trying to protect you from the unpredictable, even though it may not feel that way to you. See if you can appreciate how worry is protecting you. Once you understand its purpose, it will be easier for you to have compassion for how hard this part has worked to keep you safe. Try to develop a relationship with the part by letting it feel the presence of your Confident Self. Bring it as much comfort and reassurance as you can so that it doesn't feel all alone, and see if it can relax. You can use this practice with any strong ego part that pirates your life and eclipses the Confident Self.

Living the Practice of the Unmade Mind

Expecting problems, discontent, and unhappiness brings you exactly that: problems, discontent, and unhappiness. Expecting smooth sailing, contentment, and happiness will fill your life with these positive aspects. Try asking your old illusions to step aside, and see if you can approach situations with a more open mind. Give yourself the gift of letting the situation speak for itself, opening your mind to new and ever-expanding possibilities, instead of making it into something it might not be. The unmade mind allows you to see your life more clearly for what it is, instead of what you think it is. The unmade mind has bursts of creativity. It found a cure for polio, painted the Sistine Chapel, and put humans on the moon. The unmade mind can carry you to greater heights of personal awareness, contentment, and confidence.

Unmaking the Made-Up Mind

You can put the Practice of the Unmade Mind into use every day. Start with the awareness that we tend to approach situations with a mind-set that directs us to see whatever we're looking for. This seems like a very simple idea, but don't let its simplicity obscure its power and far-reaching possibilities in your life. If an upcoming experience starts with your mind-set, you can start to change just about anything by unmaking how you think about it and keeping your mind open to it. Here are two ways to put this practice into action:

1. Start with a made-up thought that stands in your way. Practicing separation from the thought, befriending it, and offering it comfort can create space for unmade thoughts (Confident Self) to emerge. For example, the

thought *If I leave this awful job, I'll never find one that pays as well* can be unmade into *I can find a job that I enjoy, that challenges my abilities, and that pays well.* It is possible for other unmade thoughts to appear for the made-up thoughts to consider. Write down the new thoughts. Put them where you can see them, and say them silently to yourself often, while remembering that it's not what life deals you that shapes your confidence; rather, it's your unmade mind about what life deals you that makes the difference.

2. Think about the adage "Expectations are premeditated resentments." Then think about someone you dread being around in the future. Ask yourself if you've already decided the outcome and are already having a negative or resentful reaction before the event has even occurred. Then meditate on the *dread part* of you and see if you can get it to step aside or relax and let your Confident Self lead the way while dread stays in the background during the upcoming situation. After the event, notice if your Confident Self was on the front lines and if your experience of the situation was any different than you'd previously thought.

Self-Fulfilling Imaging

According to Shakti Gawain in her book *Creative Visualization*:

Simply having an idea or thought, holding it in your mind, is an energy which will tend to attract and create that form on the material plane. If you constantly think of illness, you eventually become ill, if you believe yourself to be beautiful, you become so.[3]

The following practice of visualizing your Confident Self holding or being with an ego part can help you reflect on positive outcomes and create them in your life:

Sit in a comfortable position in a place where you won't be distracted for five or ten minutes. Close your eyes and focus on your breathing. Breathe in through the nose and out through the mouth several times. Let your body relax completely. Continue breathing and relaxing until you are in a relaxed state. See if you can immerse yourself in your Confident Self. Meditate on something you'd like to see happen in your life. See the desired outcome actually coming true in your mind's eye. See your Confident Self in situations where you expect the positive outcome to happen. See it happening vividly and imagine the smallest details of the event. Be curious about what parts of you get triggered as you imagine something happening as you would want it. Notice and honor any parts—such as doubt or skepticism that pop up with concerns about what you're imagining. Just let them be there and watch them as you continue imagining. Welcome all your parts, even resistance. Reassure them that all you're doing is imagining. Invite them to hang out and imagine with you.

After visualizing what you want several times in as many different ways as you can, open your eyes and state the desired outcome several times as if it is already taking place. Write it down two or three times, and see it in print: I am now experiencing . . .

Repeat this exercise as often as necessary.

Regardless of whether you take a metaphysical or scientific approach, the outcome can be the same when you have confident expectations. You might imagine a satisfying job, a healthy relationship, a successful golf game, a new house, inner serenity, or greater prosperity. Name and visualize your desires as vividly as you can. Imagine your expectations already coming true in your mind. Create these confident outcomes, visualize them often, and don't let them go. Our thoughts can become reality when we give them positive energy and work collaboratively with our ego parts to experience them as if they are already coming true. If the desired outcome doesn't occur, check to see if parts of your conditioned mind could be standing in the way. If so, work curiously and compassionately with those parts in the ways described in previous chapters.

Chapter Nine

The Practice of the Vacuum

Moving out of your life what you don't want to make room for what you do want

Nature does abhor a vacuum, and when you begin moving out of your life what you do not want, you automatically are making way for what you do want.

—Catherine Ponder

Hanging On for Dear Life

Jenny invited her best friend to come live with her, her husband, and their two children. During the course of the next year, Jenny kept house, did all the cooking, and remained a good mother and wife. She was delighted that her girlfriend could become part of her family, but the generous offer turned sour when Jenny discovered that her girlfriend had been sleeping with her husband. Her husband and best friend moved away and married, leaving Jenny with an emptiness that quickly filled with bitterness, resentment, and anger toward the two people who had been her closest allies.

Holding on to those negative feelings for the next three years actually caused Jenny more pain and hurt than the two people who hurt her. The husband and girlfriend had begun a happy life in another city and weren't affected by Jenny's stored-up rage, but Jenny was miserable. She suffered the emotional and physical consequences of carrying those stored feelings for years. She lost too much weight, couldn't sleep, wasn't as productive at her job, and started taking antidepressants. She reasoned that if she couldn't have her husband, she could at least have her anger and bitterness, which gave her something to hold on to. If she gave that up, she would have lost everything, or so she thought.

Many of us are more accustomed to holding on to what we want than we are of letting it go. Our way of life teaches us to possess rather than give, not only with material things but also with feelings. If we get something, we win. If we give up something, we lose. So we are more likely to possess, own, accumulate, cling, and take than we are to give up and let go. In the words of David Richo, "The ego loves to grab and cling but finds only disquietude and disappointment that way. We let go so we can be happy. Letting go is not a loss but an emancipation."[1]

Hoarding money, for example, keeps us poverty stricken because it closes us down. Spending it wisely and making donations to worthy causes create a vacuum that opens a channel for prosperity to flow back. As good comes to us, we must let go of it to keep it coming. Letting it go maintains a vacuum for more to enter. We cannot prosper if we hoard things or feelings like we would cage an animal. The traits of hoarding, possessing, and selfishness block the channels of receptivity. In other words, a closed fist cannot receive a gift. "Go with the flow" literally means tapping into currents of energy that move and flow around us and riding those magnetic waves in the direction they're going.

To make room for what makes our lives run more smoothly, according to the Practice of the Vacuum, we can move out of our lives whatever prevents them from working. This practice operates in terms of our external and internal worlds. Nature abhors a vacuum and quickly fills one up on the physical or emotional plane.

When you create a vacuum by getting rid of material things that are broken down or obsolete, you automatically create a space for something better to fill it up. Suppose you want money for a new wardrobe, but your closets are over-flowing with old clothes. The money will not manifest until you get rid of the old clothes that are tattered and torn and no longer fit. By doing so, you create a vacuum and open the way for the money and new wardrobe to come into your life.

When you unburden the thoughts or feelings that are

blocking confidence, you create a space for a more Confident Life. Suppose you want a happier life but your ego is cluttered with negativity that no longer serves the happy lifestyle you seek. Separating the cluttered thoughts and observing them with curiosity makes room for your Confident Self to take the reigns. The Practice of the Vacuum asks you to gain an understanding of the old, the familiar, and the things, people, and attitudes that you have outgrown or clung to out of fear. The clinging part is usually fear based, and befriending it can help it relax, which, in turn, can create an inner space or vacuum. Once you have a vacuum, you have an open current for clarity, calm, and confidence to fill your life.

A coworker stabs you in the back at the office, foiling your success on a project. A neighbor ridicules you for an honest mistake, or a loved one humiliates you in front of other family members. You can still feel the stinging hurt and the betrayal. The memory is as fresh as yesterday, the pain so heavy your heart aches. Hanging on to resentment seems like the natural way to get sweet revenge. It's a way to punish the wrongdoer for what they did. The thought of letting go of resentment is out of the question. Giving up your grudges and resentments might unleash a groundswell of emotions like a bursting dam, and there would be no way to retaliate. "Why should Jenny forgive her husband and best friend?" you might explode. "They did a horrible thing to her!" Yes, it was a selfish, hurtful thing for someone to do, but the truth is that holding grudges keeps the hurtful situation at the center of your daily experience and keeps you emotionally imprisoned by it.

Holding grudges takes a lot of emotional energy that could be used in more positive ways that would bring greater benefits. There's an old saying that those who anger you conquer you. Carrying a chip on your shoulder only hurts you, weighing you down, sometimes morphing into depression. So releasing resentments is for Jenny's sake, not for her husband or girlfriend. It is a loving, compassionate act for her to do for herself.

Physician and author Bernie Siegel has said that we store our childhoods inside our bodies and that once we're grown our body collects the bill.[2] Harboring anger and resentment can cause a chemical reaction inside our bodies. Unhealthy feelings are transformed into negative chemical reactions that manifest into serious physical illness. If we don't release these toxic thoughts and feelings, they can cause disease, prompt weight gain, and, in some cases, destroy us. If we keep ignoring our needs, our bodies hear the message that we don't care about ourselves, and it helps us die.

You don't have to be a rocket scientist to know that headaches, certain body pain, palpitations, nausea, and other physical symptoms often come from storage of our emotions in the body. Unless we create a vacuum for the damaged goods, they can fester and eventually cause us great physical and mental harm.

Creating a Vacuum from the Inside Out

When I first started thinking about moving away from the bustling city life to a small mountain town, several of my colleagues and friends warned, "You'll never get a private practice off the ground because that small town is saturated with psychotherapists."

I listened to them but kept the advice at arm's length so that my self-doubt didn't steamroll over my Confident Self to make the decision. In other words, I reserved an inner space for clarity and confidence to make the decision, not the doubtful part of me originating from my past and other people's fears. Employing the Practice of the Vacuum from the inside out paid off. I made the move and established a successful practice and still live and work in that small town today.

To lead a Confident Life, it is important to discover what is blocking (or protecting) us on the inside from leading one. Suppose you want healthier relationships, but your life is crowded with unhealthy friends. You must first let go of the unhealthy relationships to make room for healthier people. You can do this by taking an inner inventory to determine what is in the way. You can ask yourself, "What part of me is blocking or resisting the creation of a vacuum for healthy change?"

Jude said he wanted to find his soul mate, settle down, and have kids. This sounds reasonable, and he was a good looking enough, likable, intelligent man. The problem was that he was in a relationship with a woman whom he liked but didn't love. He couldn't envision the two of them with a future together, but she loved him and he liked the feeling of being loved by someone. Despite the fact that the couple was together 24/7, Jude couldn't understand why he couldn't find Ms. Right. Until he created a vacuum for another relationship (released his girlfriend for her sake as well as his), Ms. Right wasn't going to show up.

When he inventoried his internal boardroom, Jude became acquainted with a part of him blocking change in his life. It was a part of him that feared that if he let his current girlfriend go, there'd never be another woman who'd love him the way she did. He listened with compassion to the fearful part, understood its origins, and had his CEO (Confident Self) reassure the part by helping it see the possibility that he could feel safe *and* have a fulfilling relationship in which love was reciprocal.

Ingrid was a successful workaholic attorney, making loads of money, but her heart wasn't in it. What she really wanted was a husband and kids, but so far that hadn't happened for her. Why? She'd completely abandoned her social life in favor of working 24/7 and had unwittingly blocked any opportunity to realize the future life she hoped to achieve. When new clients called, she resented them, as if they were intruding into her personal life, taking her further away from her dream. Potential clients started to complain about her belligerent attitude.

On the surface, Ingrid's actions might seem absurd. She had marketed herself in the phone books, by word of mouth, and with a shingle hanging outside her office. The phone was ringing off the hook, which is exactly what she had worked toward, but her ego parts were leading her life. Instead of being true to herself about what she wanted, a driven part of her eclipsed her Confident Self. The driven part—not her clients—took her in the direction opposite from where she wanted to go, and a resentful part emerged in reaction to the driven part.

Ingrid applied the Practice of the Vacuum by developing a relationship with the resentful part of her, promising to start taking more time off for a social life if it would step aside and relax with new clients. As the resentment relaxed, it created a vacuum for her to step into the front lines, where she was more welcoming of clients. She also got her driven part to relax by reminding it that she could continue to be successful and have a personal life, too. As both her resentful and driven parts stepped back from leading her life, they created a vacuum for her Confident Self to take over the reigns. Ingrid started leaving work at six o'clock and reserving weekends and holidays for fun. She went out with friends and put herself into situations where she could meet new people. She eventually married, had kids, and continued a successful law practice.

Phil's restaurant business was falling apart because of his lackadaisical managerial style. He was a nice guy, salt of the earth—such a nice guy, in fact, that he couldn't say no to employees. He wanted people to like him, so if a server was late or the chef didn't show, Phil's response was "No big deal. I'll fill in." Eventually, the stress and chaos of no-shows, tardiness, early departures, and two-hour lunch breaks took their toll.

Phil was angry that employees took advantage of his kind nature. The problem was that his approval part, not his Confident Self, was running the restaurant. Approval might get people to like us, but approval alone cannot create a well-run establishment. Phil was forced to decide which was more important: being liked or having a solid business. Once he explored and understood his approval part, it relaxed, creating a vacuum for his Confident Self to manage what became a tighter ship. Plus, he was able to make the shift in a way that employees continued to like him and actually to respect him even more. That's because the Confident Self has inherent qualities that connect us to people without the need for approval.

Letting Go for Dear Life

The Practice of the Vacuum shows that the parts of yourself that seem to cause harm or to stand in your way—animosity, anger, fear, worry, jealousy, hurt, depression—will release if you're willing to establish understanding relationships with them. As long as you're a storehouse for illusions that no longer serve you, there is no space for your Confident Self who, eclipsed by your illusions, remains in the background. You can walk around resentful or unhappy much of the time and not even understand why.

Gary Zukav, in his book *The Seat of the Soul,* insists that we have a multitude of different currents inside ourselves. He says we learn to experience the energy of our soul when our personality "learns to value and to identify with those currents that generate creativity, healing and love, and to challenge and release those currents that create negativity, disharmony and violence." He goes on to say:

> When we align our thoughts, emotions, and actions with the highest part of ourselves, we are filled with enthusiasm, purpose, and meaning. Life is rich and full. We have no thoughts of bitterness. We have no memory of fear. We are joyously and intimately engaged with our world.[3]

Love, compassion, clarity, and the other six C's are qualities of the soul that can be eclipsed by old hurts. Releasing old hurts unburdens us, taking that weight off our shoulders. Once we've released the old, we are ready to receive the new. Letting go opens our spiritual channels, letting the negative flow out and the positive flow in.

Many techniques are available for creating an inner vacuum and opening the channels of flow. Using your internal boardroom and developing relationships with parts that block the back-and-forth flow constitute the most heralded approach in this book.

The following cathartic practices can help you access ego parts so that you can begin to understand them and get them to relax enough so that your Confident Self can align with them.

- Talking to a trusted friend or trained therapist can help get the flow moving.
- Support groups, such as Twelve-Step programs, can help you talk out thoughts and feelings in a caring atmosphere.
- Keeping a journal or diary, writing your thoughts down, or talking them into a recorder gets the flow moving outward.
- Employing any type of creative outlet, such as art, drama, music, or poetry, can help with the constructive expression of ego parts.
- Venting strong feelings of rage through such constructive methods as pounding clay, batting a punching bag, or hitting your mattress gives strong parts an avenue of expression—crying, screaming, banging, and laughing in controlled circumstances allow parts to release their energy.
- Exercising—such as running, aerobics, fast walking, or sports activities—enables us to work out frustration, anger, and other parts of ourselves that need expression.
- Using release meditations is another method of unclogging emotional channels. Release meditations can help

you let go of feelings or fixed ideas, attitudes, and opinions of what form, shape, and solution a troublesome situation "should take."

Burying the Hatchet for Your Sake

The only true way to put the past behind you is to remember and forgive, for remembering and forgiving help you let go. Forgetting—which you really cannot do anyway—is a form of resistance. Forgiving others for wrong actions is the ultimate act of Self-love because you do it for your benefit, not for the person who wronged you. You can set yourself free by forgiving the person who wronged you and releasing the resentments one by one. Forgiveness forms a vacuum that can be filled with a sense of calm, clarity, and confidence.

Are you being harmed or helped by holding on to long-term resentment or anger? Would you be harmed or helped by letting it go? If you're being harmed, it may be time for your own sake to forgive someone for what they did to you. By forgiving the wrongful acts of someone toward whom you've harbored negative thoughts and feelings, you conquer them, because you are no longer dominated by what they did. You free yourself from the unhealthy feelings. This letting go brings you a calm and softer heart. But don't forgive someone if your heart isn't in it. The writer Sidney Harris once said, "There's no point in burying a hatchet if you're going to put up a marker on the site." You have to be honestly ready and willing to let go of the anger, hurt, and self-pity to fully release it.

This exercise gives you hands-on experience in burying the hatchet for good—not only for past transgressions but for anything that will happen in the future. Think of a person (including yourself) toward whom you have felt hurt or resentment—someone whom you have condemned, criticized, or treated unkindly. This can be someone who did something you didn't like or someone who gets under your skin for simply being "chronically who they are"—such as a parent who constantly puts you down or a partner who always looks for the negative.

Establish a friendly connection with your resentment part, letting it know you can see its point of view and helping it see how forgiveness can benefit it. Continue with understanding and empathy until the resentment part is ready to forgive the offender *entirely* and *completely,* even for things he or she has yet to do or will continue to do. Make sure the resentment is willing to forgive the offender *totally* for all past, present, and future transgressions. Once the resentment part can truthfully answer yes, write down on a sheet of paper this offender's name and what he or she did or does that arouses your strong feelings. Close your eyes and imagine yourself talking with this person. Visualize him or her doing whatever it is that bothers you.

Next, see yourself forgiving that offender *completely.* After you feel true forgiveness in your heart, open your eyes, tear the paper into tiny pieces, and throw it into the trash bin. The next time resentment toward the offender bubbles up, thank the resentment part for sharing, and remind it that you've already forgiven this person.

An affirmation by Catherine Ponder is an example of a forgiveness meditation. You can repeat it as often as needed to release negative feelings toward someone who harmed you, whom you dislike, or with whom you feel in some way out of harmony. Try practicing it for fifteen minutes each day:

> *I fully and freely forgive you. I loose you and let you go. So far as I am concerned that incident between us is finished forever. I do not wish to hurt you. I wish you no harm. I am free and you are free and all is well again between us.*[4]

Forgiving yourself or others creates the vacuum that will unburden your resentments. If you have been self-critical or have criticized others, the meditation can get the critical part to relax. After the meditation, ask yourself what qualities of the Confident Self you'd like to fill that space. The following is another release meditation that you can use to let go of upsetting thoughts or feelings:

> *I release, one by one, all the upsetting thoughts and feelings that I have carried and that have weighed heavily on my mind and heart. I wish you no harm. I bury the hatchet once and for all and set myself free. As these burdens lift, I am open to receiving life's blessings in this empty space.*

Living the Practice of the Vacuum

Living the Practice of the Vacuum helps you create a mass exodus of thoughts or feelings that keep you trapped. Once the ego parts blocking your Confident Self have more trust in you, they will relax and create a space for other qualities you'd like to invite in to bring more balance to your life.

The Good-bye Exercise

It is impossible to bring yourself fully into a new relationship, experience, job, or period of life until you have fully said good-bye to the old. This exercise can be used to help truly leave a relationship, an old job, old ways of doing things, or a period of life, or it can be used in periods of ambivalence as a catalyst to remember what was sacred about something you're leaving and rekindle your desire to recommit to it.

Complete each of the questions and statements on pages 172–173:

THE GOOD-BYE EXERCISE

1. What was it like being in a relationship with (the person, place, or thing)?

_____

_____

_____

_____

2. Name each negative experience you had, and after each say *I say good-bye to that.*

_____

_____

_____

_____

3. Name the resentments you carry for all of this, and after each say *I say good-bye to that.*

_____

_____

_____

_____

4. Name each positive experience you had, and after each say *I say good-bye to that.*

_____

_____

_____

_____

5. Name the fondness you carry for all of this, and after each say *I say good-bye to that.*

_____

_____

_____

_____

6. Name each dream you held for this relationship, and after each say *I say good-bye to that.*

_____

_____

_____

_____

7. Finally say, *I am releasing myself from my past with you, and I am getting ready to enter my future.*

   You may need to go through this exercise more than once until you are able to completely let go of the old and create a space to bring in the new relationship, job, experience, or period of your life. Once you feel you've created a vacuum, complete the final statement:

8. And I say "HELLO" to:

_____

_____

_____

_____

_____

_____

Removing Roadblocks

The exercise below can give you a deeper understanding of something inside of you standing in the way of your life moving forward.[5] Using any art media you desire, make the following four drawings, each on a separate sheet of paper. Your artistic ability doesn't matter. You can use stick drawings or abstract symbols. Take as much time as you need.

REMOVING ROADBLOCKS

1. **Draw the Problem.** Think of a roadblock or problem that you'd like to change or move out of your life. How does that problem feel inside of you? Draw how it feels. If the problem is with your partner, don't draw his or her face yelling at you. Draw how it feels on the inside when he or she yells at you. Once you've completed the first drawing, jot down any words, thoughts, feelings, and beliefs that go with this problem.

2. **Draw the Resolution.** If this problem were resolved just the way you want, how would it feel inside of you? Draw how the resolution would feel inside of you, not your partner's smiling face. Then, jot down any words, thoughts, feelings, and beliefs that go with this resolution.

3. **Draw the Block.** What's inside of you that blocks you from going from the problem to the resolution? Draw how that block feels inside of you, not your partner pointing his or her finger at you. Again, jot down words, thoughts, feelings, and beliefs that go with this block.

4. **Draw the Release.** What needs to happen inside of you to release the block? Draw the first thing that comes to mind. Draw what this release would feel or look like on the inside. Again jot down words, thoughts, feelings, and beliefs that go with this block.

Catharsis Letter

The purpose of a catharsis letter is for your upset feelings to have a field day, instead of keeping them bottled up. This is a letter for your eyes only, not for the eyes of the person who upset you. Let the part of you that is upset hold the pen and start with "Dear (name of the person or situation)." Then start writing nonstop as fast as you can without lifting your pen off the paper. Try not to censor the upset feelings or edit the thoughts. Don't try to make sense of what you put down. Remember this letter is for you and no one else. Once you're through, put the letter in a private place or destroy it. It has already served its purpose. You can repeat this exercise again and again, addressing the same person or situation until it feels resolved. Once you feel like you've created a vacuum, ask yourself what qualities you'd like to invite into that space that the release created. Then picture those qualities filling up the vacuum, and you'll feel more like throwing a party instead of a fit.

Chapter Ten

The Practice of Magnetism

Attracting people and situations
into your life that mirror the
confident images you hold of yourself

The type of human being we prefer reveals the
contours of our heart.

—*José Ortega y Gasset*

Like Attracts Like

When I was a young college student, my confidence was
low. Looking back, I know I was smart and good-looking
enough, but at the time my illusions prevented me from
thinking of myself that way. I got invited to parties but
rarely went because I thought of myself as uninteresting and

unattractive, and I would remind myself often of those illusions. When I did push myself to go, I would unwittingly behave in ways that fit with the perceptional illusions I had of myself. I would stand on the sidelines while others laughed, danced, and had fun. Instead of joining in the fun, I waited for someone to initiate conversations, but I never really gave people a chance. Driven by self-doubt, I would look away if someone looked at me. After about an hour of this torture, I'd leave the party, reprimanding myself for going in the first place and affirming my negative illusions: "See, dumb ass, hardly a soul spoke to you all night long."

In effect, my illusions directed my actions, which confirmed my original belief about myself. Thankfully, by applying the Practice of Perception, I began to question the image through which I looked at myself, to separate from it, and to look more objectively and think more positively about myself. As I began to affirm my positive qualities and to believe them, my Confident Self took the lead and my behaviors in social situations automatically changed, too. Eventually, I completely disproved my old self-defeating perceptions, and people began responding more positively to me—a feedback loop that strengthened my confidence.

Whatever happens inside you will materialize in your daily life because whatever you think about expands. As your thoughts morph into behaviors, you attract into your life whatever you think about yourself. It all starts with the Practice of Perception. If your illusions about yourself (your parts) are running the show, the Practice of Magnetism kicks in to re-create a facsimile of people and conditions from your past. This happens on an unconscious level, but when your Confident Self is at the helm, you can create a more conscious, more confident life, quite different from your past.

I became aware of how my illusions kept me thinking and behaving in archaic ways that attracted people and conditions resembling my past. My confidence did a complete about-face when I separated on the inside from my illusions, which had eclipsed my Confident Self. As I started running my life on the inside, my outside life completely transformed into a more Confident Life. The fact is that believing in yourself and holding confident images of yourself paves the way for a Confident-Led Life.

Emily's first marriage had ended on vacation in Yosemite National Park. Basking in the warm sunshine, the clean fresh air, and the breathtaking natural beauty, she turned to share the experience with her husband, who was on his cell phone to Venezuela, grunting and kicking the dirt because he'd just lost a huge business deal. The disconnection and loneliness were painfully familiar to Emily, who worked harder and harder to make the relationship click.

Ten years after this incident, Emily and her second husband sat before me, with her marriage again on the rocks, partly for the same reasons. She felt that her husband was emotionally absent from the marriage. She wondered what was wrong with her that she couldn't keep a marriage together. "Tell me why I keep getting involved in relationships with men who use me and then suddenly pull away!" Emily demanded.

Why did she keep marrying men who were emotionally shut down? Emily realized that every romantic relationship she had ever had was with an emotionally vacant man. The distance between Emily and her husband felt deeply familiar to her because it echoed the same loneliness she had felt while growing up with an absent, workaholic father who was uninvolved in her life. She had been trying her whole life to fill that void with the only kind of relationship she knew: with emotionally distant men.

Kyle, the son of an alcoholic, declared half seriously and half jokingly, "I can be the only man in a room with a hundred women, only one of whom grew up with an alcoholic parent, and we gravitate straight toward each other in five minutes flat!"

Similar scenarios are repeated again and again in therapists' offices. We can explain this phenomenon through the Practice of Magnetism or mutual attraction: like attracts like. On a metaphysical level, this law of mutual attraction is explained through the interaction of subatomic particles that are all around us. Each of us has an energy field. We are walking, talking, electrical fields of energy that seek harmony. The frequencies of our magnetic fields are pulled in various directions toward other compatible fields of energy. We are drawn to people who have compatible energy fields. Thoughts and feelings have their own magnetic energy, which attracts energy of a similar nature. So when two adults from alcoholic homes are in a room with a hundred other people, chances are they'll gravitate toward each other.

People of a particular quality and frequency attract other people who radiate energy of a similar frequency and vibration. We attract people and situations that mirror the images we hold of ourselves. If you lack confidence, you'll attract and be attracted to people and situations that reflect a lack of confidence. When you lead from confidence, you'll attract and be attracted to confident people and situations. If you dislike yourself, you'll be attracted to others who dislike themselves and express it through unkind deeds. When you're troubled and confused, you'll be attracted to troubled, confused souls. If you're not kind to yourself, chances are that friends and loved ones won't be kind to you, either. This is the root of the old adage "Birds of a feather flock together."

All relationships start with you. How you get along with yourself sets the stage for how you'll get along with others. The better your relationship with yourself, the better it will be with others. No relationship will ever make you feel better about yourself, and no amount of people pleasing will bring self-acceptance. Another way of saying this is that Confident-Led people attract other people who lead their lives from the inside out. Conversely, people who lead their lives from their parts are attracted to other people who live from the outside in. As we become more Confident-Led and

less parts-led, we literally change the frequency and vibration of our energy fields, so that we attract and are attracted
to people who live their lives from the Confident Self.

Confident Self energy is *open* energy and vibrates at a different frequency than the energy of our parts, which is *closed*
energy. Like a tuning fork, your Confident Self energy can
trigger the vibration of Confident Self energy in someone else.
By the same token, parts energy can trigger the same energy
in another person. Skilled salespeople, for example, are trained
in handling disgruntled customers. When you're upset about a
product, a calm, empathic salesperson (one who might say, "I
can understand why you'd be upset, and I'm going to make it
right!") can diffuse your anger into calm, whereas a belligerent salesperson (one who might say, "It worked in the store.
What did you do to it?") can trigger defensive, oppositional
parts in you. Confident-Led strategies can create more
Confident Self energy between employers and employees and
within couples when they're having conflict.

A wealth of research shows that like attracts like.
Alcoholics are attracted to alcoholics, children of abuse frequently are attracted to adult abusers, and people who are
abandoned in childhood often reexperience abandonment in
adult relationships. We also know that a high incidence of
careaholics had childhoods in which they took care of
dependent parents, siblings, or other family members. It also
explains why adults, married two or three times, say they
unwittingly keep marrying the same person again and again.

Statistics indicate that adults from alcoholic homes tend to marry and become friends with other adult children from dysfunctional families, or they are attracted to and marry spouses who are codependent or alcoholic, thereby replicating the dysfunction from their upbringing. Adult children may become alcoholic, marry alcoholics, and often surround themselves with friends and coworkers who also come from dysfunctional families and who have some type of addiction to drugs, food, work, sex, relationships, and so forth.

Romantic Attraction

When Sharon did something wrong as a child, she had to win back her mother's approval. Her mother gave her the cold shoulder until she proved she could be the perfect little girl. Today, that perfect little girl is attracted to men who are psychologically unavailable. Sharon relives the relationship with her mother many times over in the men she dates, making herself a doormat to get the love and approval she never got as a little girl.

At age forty-four Phyllis was miserable, and everyone in her life seemed to contribute to her misery. Her father died of alcoholism, and her husband couldn't hold a job because of his drinking. "I continue to attract and am attracted to losers," she whined. "Why isn't my life working?"

The science behind the like-attracts-like pattern indicates that in romantic relationships your unconscious brain tries to re-create the conditions of your upbringing (good or bad) in order to correct them. Harville Hendrix developed Imago Relationship Therapy, a type of marriage therapy, around this basic idea. (*Imago* is Latin for "image.") Evidence points to the fact that romantic attraction is based on a composite picture of the people who influenced you most strongly at an early age. This Imago is a template that determines the kind of mate you'll be attracted to as an adult. When an Imago match is made deep in your brain, a surge of interest in the other person occurs. Partners in love relationships activate in each other anxieties that plunge them back into the central conflicts of their upbringing in order to have it turn out better the second time around.

Usually, in these instances, the person is unconsciously choosing someone who in some way matches their Imago without consciously realizing it. We unconsciously surround ourselves with people and situations that feel comfortable and familiar—even when we vow to avoid harmful situations, yet end up in them anyhow, fully knowing the consequences of our actions. We go back to the same people for the same rejections. We keep trying to solve problems in the same old ways that we know don't work. Why do we continue repeating the same actions, expecting different results? According to Harville Hendrix, it's the unconscious Imago at work:

> Many people have a hard time accepting the idea that they have searched for partners who resembled their caretakers. On a con-

scious level, they were looking for people with only positive traits—people who were, among other things, kind, loving, good-looking, intelligent, and creative. In fact, if they had an unhappy childhood, they may have deliberately searched for people who were radically different from their caretakers. They told themselves, "I'll never marry a drunkard like my father," or "There's no way I'm going to marry a tyrant like my mother." But, no matter what their conscious intentions, most people are attracted to mates who have their caretakers' positive and negative traits, and, typically, the negative traits are more influential.[1]

We're basically looking for people who duplicate our parents' inadequacies. The old brain is returning to the scene of the crime, so to speak, to right the wrongs of our childhoods. We expect our partners to make up for the problem, but the unfortunate consequence is that, because of the Imago match, we get rewounded.

The solution to changing this pattern of attraction is figuring out what's not working and changing it instead of repeating it. The first step is to become more conscious of what's happening inside of you when you are attracted to someone. Identify the parts of you that are looking for a relationship to heal their wounds and start giving to the wounded parts of yourself from your Confident Self what they never got. This is called *self-soothing*. Through its pure nature for compassion and connection, the Confident Self soothes the wounded part of you so that relationship choices are led by the Self instead of by the wounded part.

Emily was able to see how repeating her unhealthy

choices kept her stuck. Emotionally distant men became red flags for her. She finally connected with a man who showered her with love and attention and with whom she shared emotional responsibility for their relationship.

Living the Practice of Magnetism

Breaking your attraction to unhealthy relationships and conditions begins with your own Self-acceptance and Self-love. As you practice Self-love, unhealthy relationships and life conditions melt away. You radiate positive thoughts and feelings, and you attract and are attracted to people who are spreading the same positive energy to you.

Repeat Offender

Are you a repeat offender in your personal life? If so, identify your thoughts or parts or actions that eclipse your Confident Self on the inside. Identify what you keep doing that causes you to attract people and conditions that keep your confidence from leading. Next, applying the practices described in previous chapters, take a different direction from the inside out and the outside in that you haven't tried before.

Magnetism Meditation

Think of yourself as an irresistible magnet, capable of attracting all the good that surrounds you. Think healthy, positive thoughts about yourself and others. Send yourself positive messages that affirm you. Name the qualities about yourself and the blessings in your life for which you're grateful. Focus on your abundance, instead of your lack. Think only good things happening for everyone you know — those closest to you and even those with whom you feel at odds. Radiate positive thoughts and feelings. Fill your mind with healthy thoughts and imagine good things for yourself. As you radiate positive thoughts, visualize positive things drawn toward you. See yourself attracting whatever you radiate with the following affirmation:

I am a healthy, loving, happy person, and I attract healthy, loving, and happy people and situations.

When realized from the Confident Self, the following meditation from Catherine Ponder reinforces the Practice of Magnetism:

I am an irresistible magnet, with the power to attract unto myself everything that I divinely desire, according to the thoughts, feelings and mental pictures I constantly entertain and radiate. I am the center of my universe! I have the power to create whatever I wish. I attract whatever I radiate. I attract whatever I mentally choose and accept. I begin choosing and mentally accepting the highest and best in life. I now choose and accept health, success and happiness. I now choose lavish abundance for myself and for all mankind. This is a rich, friendly universe and I dare to accept its riches, its hospitality, and to enjoy them now![2]

Your Magnetogram

Think of up to eight important people in your life: your spouse/partner/love interest, coworkers, friends, parents, children, or others. On Figure 10.1, write their names in the circles around the *You* circle. Next, draw a line symbolizing the nature of your relationship with each person. Straight lines represent solid, healthy relationships; jagged lines, bumpy or shaky relationships; spirals, confused or uncertain relationships.

Figure 10.1: Your Magnetogram

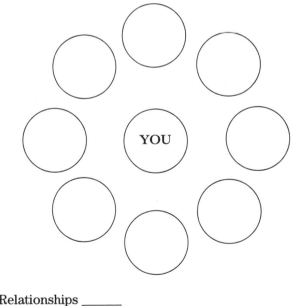

Solid Relationships _____
Bumpy Relationships
Uncertain Relationships ℓℓℓℓℓℓℓℓℓℓℓℓℓ

After you've completed the magnetogram ask yourself the following questions:

1. What does this diagram tell you about you and your relationships?
2. What kinds of people surround you in your life?
3. Do they affirm and support your confidence or undermine it?
4. What clues do you see about how your life is being led from the inside?
5. What relationship patterns within you or between you and another person would you like to change?
6. What ego parts are standing in the way that need your attention, appreciation, and understanding before your relationships can improve?
7. With the Confident Self leading, see if you can meet the emotional needs of all the parts you have identified in the preceding questions by providing the parts with the self-soothing and loving-kindness they never got when you were younger.

Chapter Eleven

The Practice of the Boomerang

*Projecting confidence from within
that will come back into your life
in one form or another*

I have found that if you love life, life will love you
back.

— *Arthur Rubinstein*

The Looking Glass

*M*any years ago, I was so excited I could hardly stand
it. I was on my way to become enlightened!
Winding through the North Carolina mountains, my little
car puttered its way to a Buddhist retreat center nestled in
the Great Smoky Mountains, located near the border of

North Carolina and Tennessee. Although I'd heard about the wonderful teachings, I hadn't had a chance to learn or practice them firsthand because my life was so busy, but this weekend would be different. I'd devote two whole days, along with other seekers, sitting cross-legged, meditating, chanting mantras, and contemplating the universe. I figured I'd find inner peace, and all of life's secrets would be revealed to me in one fell swoop. Who wouldn't be excited? I was on my way to becoming a "Higher Being"! A longtime friend had told me about this retreat center and had advised me that my experience there would mirror my everyday life.

Yeah, right! I remember thinking, waving him away, *Gimme a break!*

My life was so stressful and out of control—I was looking for inner peace and direction. After all, isn't that what retreat centers are for: to bathe you in inner peace? I'd be an idiot to go somewhere for more of the same.

But there I was—lost. Snaking around the treacherous curves, I realized I'd misjudged the time it would take for the three-hour trip. Having started late, I hadn't left work early enough to beat the darkness. It was nightfall, and I could hardly see the tiny, unmarked dirt road that curved ahead of me. I had left my eyeglasses on an airplane earlier in the week, and it had started to rain. I was already two hours late to have dinner and assemble with the monk who would give us instructions for the weekend. Angry and frustrated, I cursed the darkness and beat the steering wheel. *If only I hadn't waited so long to leave!*

Hungry and exhausted, I finally saw the sign for the retreat center. Once inside, I was informed that the other participants had already eaten and were assembling for instructions. I scarfed down a bowl of soup and piece of bread and dashed to the assembly and plopped into my seat, the last to be seated. I was out of breath, my heart was pounding, and my hands were shaking. My unpacked bags waited patiently in the car trunk, and, although the others had settled into their rooms, I was homeless. At that moment the monk announced that there would be no talking for twenty-four hours under any circumstances. My heart sank, and my stomach pole-vaulted in marked contrast to the instant calm I'd expected. *When does the inner peace begin?* I grumbled to myself.

When I look back now, I realize my friend was right. My experience at the retreat center was a mirror for me to see myself more clearly and how I was leading my life. Before I had even gotten to the center, the "mirror" said, *I can't see and I'm lost—not just in the mountainous roads but on my life's journey.* Looking back, I could see that my old familiar friends— hurry, frustration, and anger—had carpooled with me on the trip. Sitting before the monk when he announced silence, I started to realize that two other frequent companions, anxiety and worry, also accompanied me. As painful as it was, I had been enlightened, but I didn't know it at the time.

Situations—especially challenging ones—are mirrors for you to learn from, too. You cannot love or hate something about an experience unless it reflects to you something you love or hate about yourself. This is the Practice of the Boomerang, which also holds true how you react to other people. When you react negatively to someone, it is usually an ego part reacting to something that it doesn't like within you. It has been said that the faults of others are like automobile headlights: they always seem more glaring than our own. Many of us have become experts at evaluating and judging others because it keeps the spotlight off us. The fact is that the defects we point out in others are usually the very things we don't like about ourselves. Focusing on the faults of others is simply a way to distract ourselves from acknowledging that those same traits also exist in us and prevent us from seeing what we need to work on in ourselves.

The psychologist Carl Jung once said, "Everything that irritates us about others can lead us to an understanding of ourselves." Sometimes you might catch your ego (or parts) on a fault-finding mission. Once you step back, you can see that it's usually something within yourself about which you're displeased. Criticizing someone else is just a way to feel better inside. If we can highlight others' flaws, it makes ours more tolerable or perhaps even makes us feel superior.

The Practice of the Boomerang teaches you to catch yourself when you want to judge someone else and to notice what the criticism mirrors about you. Then you can harness the energy you would use to criticize that person and put it to good use by working on that part of yourself. Once you've mastered this strategy, you can practice favor finding instead of fault finding and notice how much better it feels to elevate others instead of putting them down. This approach gives the other person due credit, and you have the opportunity to gain better understanding, compassion, and a greater capacity for confidence.

The Practice of the Boomerang says that whatever is going on inside of us gets projected into our outer worlds and comes back as a mirror for change for us to look into, if we are willing. All thoughts, feelings, and actions that we put out come back in some form. Sending out positive thoughts, feelings, and actions causes positive experiences to come back to us. If we think ugly, hateful thoughts, then ugly, hateful things happen to us, perhaps not right away, but they will manifest in our lives eventually.

Such is the case with envy. Claire felt cheated when good things happened to other people. A stroke of luck for someone else was a slap in her face. She constantly complained about a coworker always bragging about the accomplishments of his children and how great his life was. "I don't want to hear all that stuff," Claire snapped. "It just makes me feel like my life's nothing!"

When a friend told Claire about her good fortune, Claire pinched her face into an ugly frown, as if she were physically sick. "Why do you always have the good luck?" she snorted, stomping her foot. "How come it always has to be you? Why couldn't it be me?"

Claire couldn't see that her envy was eclipsing a Confident Life. Her bitterness ricocheted back to her, manifesting in a lackluster life. In the words of French humanitarian Jean Vanier, "Envy comes from people's ignorance of, or lack of belief in, their own gifts." The good fortunes of others were reminders of Claire's own inner unhappiness and lack of confidence. Until she could celebrate the good fortunes of others, Claire was blind to her own gifts because they remained eclipsed by bitterness over her own life choices.

Envying what others have can keep you from seeing your own blessings and can prevent you from realizing that you have other gifts that they don't. Envy and jealousy are parts of the ego, trying to get you what you don't have, but in so doing, they unwittingly increase your feelings of poverty. When they hijack the leadership of your life, they expand and you project them into the world where they ricochet back in the form of an impoverished life. Confidence comes from being grateful for what you have—not from wanting what others have—and taking necessary steps inside out to create the choices you want. When you genuinely experience the joy of someone's good fortune, a curious thing happens: you suddenly have good fortune, too, because you're sharing in their feelings, instead of separating yourself by hoarding bitterness. When you participate in joy, you feel the joy! When you pound a table, stomp your foot, or harbor bitterness, it makes you feel bad, and you've just been boomeranged and don't even know it.

The author Shakti Gawain wrote:

> Whatever you try to create for another will always boomerang back to you. That includes both loving, helpful or healing actions and negative destructive ones.[1]

The more we use our thoughts, feelings, and actions to love ourselves and others and do kind deeds, the more love, happiness, and prosperity we will receive. The Practice of the Boomerang holds that changing negative and destructive thoughts, words, and actions into constructive ones yields positive life experiences.

I am reminded of a vacation during which I shopped at a natural food store and struck up a conversation with the owner. What started off as a great chat ended in my being overbearing and critical of a concert pianist whom both of us had seen perform recently. To my astonishment I found myself counter each of her accolades with unbridled criticism. Although I didn't like what I heard coming out of my mouth, I couldn't stop the litany of negatives. Suddenly, the energy between us shifted, and the free-flowing, lighthearted conversation turned stone cold. Her smiles and laughter died, replaced by downturned lips. Fond glances turned into blank stares. The negativity I'd put out in the grocery store came thundering back to me from the owner, who had totally disconnected. I carried an unsettled feeling about my unfair judgments for the remainder of the day.

One Is a Whole Number

Metaphysicians say that we are all one vast energy source. We are all interconnected, as is everything in the universe. No matter how hard we try to be separate and individual, we're linked to the whole. We are all one great mass of subatomic particles, each with our own electromagnetic energy field.

The concept of oneness has credibility in scientific circles. Physicists claim that when atoms within a molecule align in a certain way and a critical number is reached, the rest of the atoms spontaneously line up the same way. When enough people agree on what is real — once a critical mass is reached — everyone will see reality similarly. As the critical mass of a species thinks and acts in a certain way, the remainder of the species will follow suit. The psychologist Carl Jung spoke of the "collective unconscious" that links each of us with the rest of the people in the world, influencing one another in subconscious ways.

Taoism speaks of the *yin* and *yang*, the opposites in life — good and bad, love and hate, joy and sadness, masculine and feminine — that represent the interconnectedness, harmony, and transformation of everything. The yin and yang of water, for example, are that water is both powerful and soft

at the same time. It takes life, and it gives life. The sound of
its trickle soothes us, and its cool pure taste refreshes us on
a hot day. Our bodies require water to survive. Yet over time
the powerful force of water can cut through rock and carve
ravines as long and deep as the Grand Canyon. The force of
water can generate electricity, and the force of its floods can
destroy property and even life. Thus the yin and yang of
water illustrate that it is simultaneously life sustaining and
life threatening, that even the opposites in life are one and
the same.

David Richo described the two-handed practice, which
allows you to hold the opposites of a predicament as a witness, not as plaintiff or judge:

> I lose my job and am depressed and scared. At the same time, I
> know I have to search for another job. I hold my unemployed situa-
> tion in one hand with serene acceptance of the reality of loss. I hold
> my plan to do a job search in the other. This is how my depression,
> a given of every life from time to time, does not descend into
> despair. Holding my opposites grants me serenity and courage.[2]

The fact that both physicists and mystics endorse the concept of oneness lends support to the Practice of the
Boomerang. Therefore, if we're all one, every time we help
or hurt ourselves, we help or hurt others. By the same token,
every time we help someone else, we help ourselves, and
every time we hurt someone else, we simultaneously hurt
ourselves. The negative energy from destructive words and

actions triggers negative energy in the recipients and returns in some form to hurt us because of this oneness. Every time we send ourselves negative thoughts or put ourselves down, we transfer that self-injury into daily relationships with others. When we love ourselves first and foremost, we transfer that Self-love into caring and helping those around us. Expressions of love start with loving ourselves.

When Actions Become Boomerangs

I remember camp meetings during my childhood in the South where fireflies punctuated the dark summer sky and believers fanned away the sweltering heat as they gathered under huge tents to worship. I often peeked through slits in the tents to watch the worshipers raise their arms to the heavens, clap their hands, speak in tongues, run up and down aisles, and sometimes cut cartwheels in ecstasy as they became "slain in the spirit." I was intrigued by what my boyhood eyes saw. Little did I know that these worshipers were engaging in religious practices that were essential to their mental and physical health.

Anyone who has ever had a spiritual experience will tell you of a natural high associated with it that is often impossible to describe. These natural highs or peak experiences result from connections in the brain and can occur with prayer, meditation, contemplation, or other internal experiences. For some, it is the rush they feel from seeing a beautiful sunset. For others, it is a meaningful spiritual connection through prayer. For others, it is a heightened bliss from deep meditation or connection with a Higher Power. During Buddhist meditation, practitioners describe feelings of calm, unity, and transcendence — sensations that scientists say correspond to increased activity in the brain's frontal lobes (behind the forehead) and decreased activity in the parietal lobes at the top rear of the head.

These meaningful internal experiences may be essential for survival. They cause biochemical reactions that have special benefits for our health. Scientific studies tell us that people who have a regular spiritual practice, such as going to a church or meditation, actually live longer and healthier lives than people who don't engage in such practices.

Neuroscientists know that your mind influences every cell because thoughts activate hormones that carry information throughout your body. Think of it this way: your cells are constantly eavesdropping on your thoughts and are being changed by them. Every time you have a thought or feeling, every cell of your body creates neuropeptides, chemicals that carry information throughout your body and that directly affect you physically. Through the action of these neuropeptides, you become the recipient of your own love or joy or frustration or rage.

The stress psychologist Hans Selye long ago explained how the body manufactures its own poisons when under siege by negative emotions.[3] When you are overly stressed, for example, your brain sends that message to your body through cortisol and adrenaline, stress hormones that can wear down your immune system, making you more vulnerable to illness. Norman Cousins, in his book *Headfirst*, declared, "Scarcely anything that enters the mind doesn't find its way into the workings of the body."[4] So remember that when you angrily shake your fist at the heavens, your body ricochets harmful chemicals back to you. This is the Practice of the Boomerang.

Neuroscience confirms that our anger can make us physically sick and kill us and that our laughter can heal and sustain us. Body chemistry research indicates that positive feelings and laughter enhance the immune system by increasing the number of disease-fighting immune cells. Laughter also activates the secretion of endorphins, the body's natural pain killer, which help reduce physical pain and produce interleukins and interferons—powerful cancer-fighting enzymes. Humor and lightheartedness generally reduce stress, ease pain, foster recovery, and brighten one's outlook on life, regardless of how grim the reality. When we send out positive feelings, we get back physical benefits that can prolong and improve the quality of our lives.

Those of us who persist in angry outbursts and hostility against others are ultimately hurting ourselves according to the Practice of the Boomerang. Holding on to anger and resentment has a boomerang effect and hurts us a lot more than the ones toward whom we direct our wrath. When we harbor unresolved feelings, we literally turn them inward upon ourselves, where they ravage the nervous, digestive, cardiac, and respiratory systems. The more Confident-Led we are, the less likely the ego parts will stand in the way of a longer, happier, and healthier life.

Confidence and the Boomerang Cycle

Science also informs us that confidence, or lack of it, can be a vicious cycle. Those lacking confidence self-destruct because of negative attitudes and behaviors in the workplace. Because they are often afraid to take risks and stretch themselves, they fail to reach their full potential, or they might overstretch beyond their ability and fail. Either extreme comes from under-confident people not knowing what their capabilities are. They project this lack of confidence with their doubtful, fumbling behaviors, and peers and managers respond in kind with a lack of confidence in them.

In contrast, confident workers climb the ladder of success faster and higher. They are calculated risk takers who know their limits, and they have an optimistic belief in themselves that inspires others in the workplace. They project their confidence from within, and it cycles back into their lives in the form of accolades, respect, and promotions. Confident workers ignite confidence in others in the workplace, whereas those lacking confidence spread pessimism and ill will. The Practice of the Boomerang can work either way. Whatever we put out—confidence or lack of it—will fall back in our laps.

The key to confidence at work, home, and play is inside. Working with your Confident Self and parts so that more confidence surfaces within you will provide you with what you need to project into your career and relationships. These confident projections will come back to you in many ways to enrich your life. In the words of Catherine Ponder:

> It is up to you to choose and radiate outward through your thinking what you really wish to experience in life, rather than to get bogged down in unpleasant or failure experiences of the moment. These conditions can change as quickly as you can change your thinking about them.[5]

Chicken-and-Egg Relationships

If you're willing to open your eyes, look in your mirror, and see what's there, every experience and relationship you have can reveal important lessons for you to learn. Sally is a case in point. The same situation that upset Sally, who was insecure in her marriage, didn't upset Mildred, who was confident in hers. Sally got upset when her husband went bowling without her because, she said, "He'd rather be with his friends than me."

Mildred enjoyed the time apart and believed it was healthy for husbands and wives to have individual interests. The outside conditions were the same for both marriages: both husbands loved their wives equally, and both bowled together on Thursdays, but the two wives had two different perceptions of the same reality. Clearly, the objective reality of bowling wasn't the source of upset; Sally's perception was the cause of her upset. She blamed the outside event of her husband's bowling for her insecurities when, in fact, they came from perceptions she had developed in childhood. The way she framed the situation blocked her connectedness, which, in turn, detonated angry outbursts toward her husband. He, in turn, felt frustrated and angry because of her jealousy toward his bowling companion. This created a chicken-and-egg boomerang effect. Sally's insecurity in her marriage bounced back to her from her husband. Mildred, who projected confidence in her marriage, had that same confidence boomerang back to her.

Most couples who have come to me for marriage therapy describe some type of chicken-and-egg cycle that they cannot see, understand, or break. The Practice of the Boomerang says you can change negative cycles into positive ones so that more confidence will come back to you. Sally began to understand, through the Practice of Perception, that her filter of the situation contributed to her feelings of rejection. Working inwardly—by developing a relationship between her insecure part and Confident Self and assuming a healthier, more objective outlook—helped Sally feel more secure and less resentful toward her husband. Sally's different attitude caused her husband to treat her in a more lovable way that made her feel more secure. Sally resolved the dilemma by reframing *her* perception of the situation instead of insisting that her husband give up bowling.

Living the Practice of the Boomerang

We do not send out positive energy for the sole purpose of getting something in return. We follow the Practice of the Boomerang because of genuine Self-love and love for others. You can live the Practice of the Boomerang by putting forth good without regard for material gain and by holding all your opposites as one.

The Two-Handed Practice

David Richo described the two-handed practice, which helps you hold the opposite parts of you in any conflicting situation:

> Hold both hands out cupped, palms upward and imagine them holding just such opposites. We feel the light and equal weight of both, since our hands are empty. We then say, for example, *I can serenely hold both my need for a relationship and my not having one right now.*[6]

Now think of a predicament in your life in which you are polarized. Imagine holding the predicament in one palm and your confidence to work through it in the other. One hand is serenely mindful; one is working with courage. When you can hold both viewpoints this way, you are accepting the Tao of the situation and are doing all you can do to work with it, instead of becoming overwhelmed and frustrated, which would block the solution.

The Boomerang Activity

In the exercise on page 208, set some personal goals in each of the four areas listed. Once you have achieved your four goals, chances are that your boomerang has already come back to you through the realization that "Giving is as fulfilling as receiving."

The Looking Glass

Write down five negative traits that you can describe in one word each about someone you dislike. Then look at your list and notice how many of those characteristics also ring true of you. Your criticisms, judgments, and complaints might expose more about you than the people you put down. They might tell you more about your own ego parts and what you could work on within yourself to build your confidence. You can also do this exercise with the positive traits you see in people you admire.

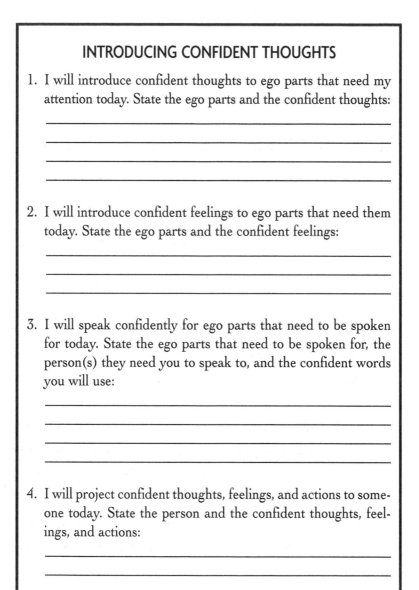

INTRODUCING CONFIDENT THOUGHTS

1. I will introduce confident thoughts to ego parts that need my attention today. State the ego parts and the confident thoughts:

   _____

   _____

   _____

   _____

2. I will introduce confident feelings to ego parts that need them today. State the ego parts and the confident feelings:

   _____

   _____

   _____

3. I will speak confidently for ego parts that need to be spoken for today. State the ego parts that need to be spoken for, the person(s) they need you to speak to, and the confident words you will use:

   _____

   _____

   _____

   _____

4. I will project confident thoughts, feelings, and actions to someone today. State the person and the confident thoughts, feelings, and actions:

   _____

   _____

   _____

❧ Conclusion ❧

Living the 10 Practices for a Life of Confidence

When you're confident from the inside out, confidence will love you back from the outside in.

— With love,
Bryan Robinson

Life is full of possibilities. It is possible for you to find your Confident Self if you peek inside with a curious, honest eye. Though no one else can imprison you, you'll see how you unconsciously erect your own self-limitations that prevent you from a Confident-Led Life. Living the 10 Practices in this book gives you a new looking-glass self that reflects the truth about you. As you live from your Confident Self, the prison bars melt away, and your confidence spreads like concentric circles on a rippling pond to your immediate circle of relationships. The outer ripples continue to touch those at work and in your circle of business associates and acquaintances. You become a shining mirror for others, helping them see their own human magnificence, and they mirror back yours, too. When you're confident from the inside out, confidence will love you back from the outside. A poem by Portia Nelson, *An Autobiography in Five Short Chapters*, can help you see which chapter best describes where your confidence is on any given day.[1]

An Autobiography

Chapter I

> *I walk down the street.*
> *There is a deep hole in the sidewalk.*
> *I fall in.*
> *I am lost . . . I am helpless.*
> > *It isn't my fault.*
> *It takes forever to find a way out.*

Chapter II

> *I walk down the same street.*
> *There is a deep hole in the sidewalk.*
> *I pretend I don't see it.*
> *I fall in again.*
> *I can't believe I am in the same place.*
> > *But, it isn't my fault.*
> *It still takes a long time to get out.*

Chapter III

I walk down the same street.
There is a deep hole in the sidewalk.
I see it is there.
I still fall in . . . it's a habit.
My eyes are open.
I know where I am.
It is my fault.
I get out immediately.

Chapter IV

I walk down the same street.
There is a deep hole in the sidewalk.
I walk around it.

Chapter V

I walk down another street.

❧ Support Organizations ❧

Beck Institute for Cognitive Therapy and Research

www.beckinstitute.org
Beck Institute for Cognitive Therapy and Research
GSB Building
City Line & Belmont Avenues
Suite 700
Bala Cynwyd, PA 19004-1610

The Beck Institute was founded in 1994 as a natural outgrowth of the psychotherapy developed by Dr. Aaron Beck, known as cognitive therapy. The center provides state-of-the-art psychotherapy and research opportunities and serves as an international training ground for cognitive therapists at all levels.

Buddhist Information and Education Network

www.buddhanet.net
Buddha Dharma Education Association, Inc.
Bodhi Tree Forest Monastery & Retreat Centre
78 Bentley Road, Tullera, via Lismore
NSW 2480 Australia

A network of Buddhist information and education, including information on Buddhist studies worldwide, a world Buddhist directory, *Buddhazine* online magazine, and book library and library resources.

Center for Self-Leadership

www.selfleadership.org

The Center for Self-Leadership

P.O. Box 3969

Oak Park, IL 60303

Established in August 2000 to promote and expand the training, consulting, clinical, and research activities of Internal Family Systems (IFS). IFS involves helping people heal by listening inside themselves in a new way to different "parts"—feelings or thoughts—and in the process, unburdening themselves of extreme beliefs, emotions, sensations, and urges that constrain their lives. This unburdening process, in particular, gives people more access to the True Self, and they are better able to lead their lives from centered, confident, compassionate places.

Imago Relationships International

www.imagotherapy.com

160 Broadway

East Building, Suite 1001

New York, NY 10038

The Institute for Imago Relationship Therapy was founded in 1984 by Harville Hendrix. Offers face-to-face learning opportunities, including national and international workshops for couples and singles, and products that teach the dynamics of the love relationship in achieving personal growth. The institute's mission is to transform marriages and relationships and to improve parenting.

Institute for Meditation and Psychotherapy

www.meditationandpsychotherapy.org

Institute for Meditation and Psychotherapy

35 Pleasant Street

Newton, MA 02459

Dedicated to the training of mental health professionals interested in the integration of mindfulness, meditation, and psychotherapy.

Kripalu Center for Yoga and Health

www.Kripalu.org

Kripalu Center for Yoga and Health

P.O. Box 309

Stockbridge, MA 01262

Offers workshops and retreats, a professional school, and an online newsletter—all designed to teach the art and science of yoga and to produce thriving and healthy individuals and society—dedicated to the inquiry of what creates a fulfilled human life.

Selected Bibliography

Chodron, Pema. 1996. *Awakening Loving-Kindness.* Boston: Shambhala. A small book to be used as a primary teacher and guide; it provides huge teachings to help readers remain wholeheartedly awake to everything in life.

Chodron, Pema. 1997. *When Things Fall Apart: Heart Advice for Difficult Times.* Boston: Shambhala. Provides ways to use painful emotions to cultivate wisdom, compassion, and courage, as well as communication that leads to openness and true intimacy with others.

Cope, Stephen. 2000. *Yoga and the Quest for the True Self.* New York: Bantam. A wonderfully written communion between Western psychotherapy and Eastern yogic philosophy for those in search of the True Self.

de Mello, Anthony. 1998. *The Way to Love: The Last Meditations of Anthony De Mello.* New York: Doubleday. Contains thirty-one meditations that encourage readers to break through illusion, which de Mello called "the great obstacle to love" as it is only when we see others as they really are that we can begin to really love.

Frankl, Viktor. 2006. *Man's Search for Meaning.* Boston: Beacon Press. Descriptions of life in Nazi death camps and its lessons for spiritual survival, exemplifying the Practice of Choice more than any other scenario of which I am aware.

Gawain, Shakti. 2002. *Creative Visualization: Use the Power of Your Imagination to Create What You Want in Your Life.* Novato, CA: New World Library. Describes the art of using mental imagery and affirmation to produce positive changes in your life.

215

Hendrix, Harville. 1988. *Getting the Love You Want: A Guide for Couples.* New York: Harper & Row. A great book on how perceptual illusions from our past (called the Imago) block our connectivity in relationships and how to overcome the obstacles.

His Holiness the Dalai Lama and Howard C. Cutler. 1998. *The Art of Happiness.* New York: Riverhead Books. Shows us how the power of an internal life strengthens us enough to navigate through whatever the external world brings us.

Ladner, Lorne. 2004. *The Lost Art of Compassion.* San Francisco: HarperCollins. Explores one of the most powerful inner resources—that of compassion—for creating a life of happiness and contentment.

Love, Patricia, and **Steve Stosny.** 2007. *How to Improve Your Marriage Without Talking About It.* New York: Broadway Books. Getting beyond talking about the relationship and finding true love through deeper connection.

Nelson, Portia. 1993. *There's a Hole in My Sidewalk: The Romance of Self-Discovery.* Hillsboro, OR: Atria Books/Beyond Words Publishing. A poetic description of the discovery of Self and the authentic feelings that come with it.

Richo, David. 2005. *The Five Things We Cannot Change . . . and the Happiness We Find by Embracing Them.* Boston: Shambhala. An excellent guide to help readers come to accept life as it is and not as they want it to be.

Robinson, Bryan. 2007. *Chained to the Desk: A Guidebook for Workaholics, Their Partners and Children, and the Clinicians Who Treat Them.* New York: New York University Press. Describes the struggle between the external life of *doing* and overdoing versus the internal life of *being*, where balance and healing are achieved.

Schwartz, Richard. 1995. *Internal Family Systems Therapy.* New York:

Guilford Press. Outlines the basic Internal Family Systems (IFS) principles for a deeper understanding of internal systems, the nature of people's subpersonalities, and how they operate as an inner ecology.

Schwartz, Richard. 2001. *Introduction to the Internal Family Systems Model.* Oak Park, IL: Trailhead Publishers. Describes Internal Family Systems (IFS), one of the fastest-growing approaches to psychotherapy, which helps people heal by listening inside themselves in a new way to different "parts." The goal is Self-leadership to overcome all obstacles in one's life.

Siegel, Daniel. 2007. *The Mindful Brain.* New York: W. W. Norton. How mindfulness promotes resonance circuits in the brain that allow us to attune to the internal lives of ourselves and others.

Tolle, Eckhart. 2004. *The Power of Now: A Guide to Spiritual Enlightenment.* Novato, CA: New World Library. A spiritual approach to inner peace that brings tranquility by leaving the analytical mind and its false created self, the ego, behind.

Tolle, Eckhart. 2005. *A New Earth: Awakening to Your Life's Purpose.* New York: Dutton. The author shows how to make the transformation within ourselves and on Earth from an ego-based life to who we truly are, which is infinitely greater than anything we currently think we are.

Welwood, John. 2006. *Perfect Love, Imperfect Relationships: Healing the Wound of the Heart.* Boston: Trumpeter. A psychospiritual approach to the root cause of all relational problems—a wounded relationship to love itself—a deep-seated suspicion many people carry within themselves that they cannot be loved or that they are not lovable, just for who they are.

‍Notes ‍

Chapter 1

1. His Holiness the Dalai Lama and Howard C. Cutler. 1998. *The Art of Happiness*. New York: Riverhead Books.
2. Dalai Lama and Cutler, *The Art of Happiness*, p. 46.
3. Fritjof Capra. 1999. *The Tao of Physics*. Boston: Shambhala, p. xix.

Chapter 2

1. Eckhart Tolle. 2005. *A New Earth: Awakening to Your Life Purpose*. New York: Dutton, p. 191.
2. Richard Schwartz. 2001. *Introduction to the Internal Family Systems Model*. Oak Park, IL: Trailhead Publishers.
3. John Gottman. 1999. *The Seven Principles for Making Marriage Work*. New York: Crown.
4. Schwartz, *Introduction to the Internal Family System Model*, p. 43.
5. Anthony de Mello. 1988. *Mastering Sadhana: On Retreat with Anthony de Mello*. New York: Doubleday, pp. 43–44.
6. Tolle, *A New Earth*, p. 30.
7. Schwartz, *Introduction to the Internal Family System Model*, pp. 43–44.
8. Pema Chodron. 1996. *Awakening Loving-Kindness*. Boston: Shambhala, p. 29.
9. Eckhart Tolle. 2004. *The Power of Now: A Guide to Spiritual Enlightenment*. Novato, CA: New World Library, pp. 18–19.
10. Schwartz, *Introduction to the Internal Family System Model*, p. 34.
11. These exercises were adapted from the work of Richard Schwartz and his Internal Family Systems Model.

Chapter 3

1. Gary Zukav. 1989. *The Seat of the Soul*. New York: Simon & Schuster, p. 206.
2. Schwartz, *Introduction to the Internal Family System Model*, p. 55.
3. Zukav, *The Seat of the Soul*, p. 208.

Chapter 4

1. Viktor Frankl. 2006. *Man's Search for Meaning*. Boston: Beacon Press.
2. Tolle, *A New Earth*, p. 274.
3. For some people, deeper work with ego parts may be necessary to practice choosing fully. This work often requires unburdening deeper parts of ourselves, called *exiles*, that have a vulnerable history—a process that is beyond the scope of this book. For further information on the unburdening process, see the work of Dr. Richard Schwartz in the Selected Bibliography section of this book.
4. This exercise was adapted from the work of Dr. Richard Schwartz and his Internal Family Systems Model.

Chapter 5

1. David Burns. 1980. *Feeling Good: The New Mood Therapy*. New York: New American Library.
2. His Holiness the Dalai Lama and Howard Cutler, *The Art of Happiness*, p. 34.
3. Jill Neimark. May/June 2007. "The Optimism Revolution," *Psychology Today*, p. 91.

Chapter 6

1. Bernie Siegel. 1986. *Love, Medicine & Miracles*. New York: Harper & Row.
2. Pema Chodron. 1997. *When Things Fall Apart: Heart Advice for Difficult Times*. Boston: Shambhala, p. 12.
3. Crystal Park, Lawrence Calhoun, and Richard Tedeschi. 1998. *Posttraumatic Growth: Positive Changes in the Aftermath of Crisis*. Mahwah, NJ: Lawrence Erlbaum.

Chapter 7

1. Emily Perl Kingsley. 1987. "Welcome to Holland." ©1987 by Emily Perl Kingsley. All rights reserved. Used with permission of the author.
2. Anthony de Mello. 1991. *The Way to Love: The Last Meditations of Anthony de Mello*. New York: Doubleday, p. 21.
3. David Richo. 2005. *The Five Things We Cannot Change . . . and the Happiness We Find by Embracing Them*. Boston: Shambhala, p. 14.

Chapter 8

1. Joseph Murphy. 1968. *The Cosmic Power Within You.* West Nyack, NY: Parker Publishers.
2. Robert Rosenthal and D. B. Rubin. 1978. "Interpersonal Expectancy Effects: The First 345 Studies." *The Behavioural and Brain Sciences,* vol. III.
3. Shakti Gawain. 2002. *Creative Visualization: Use the Power of Your Imagination to Create What You Want in Your Life.* Novato, CA: New World Library.

Chapter 9

1. Richo, *The Five Things We Cannot Change,* p. 14.
2. Siegel, *Love, Medicine & Miracles.*
3. Zukav, *The Seat of the Soul,* p. 26.
4. Catherine Ponder. 1962. *The Dynamic Laws of Prosperity.* Englewood Cliffs, NJ: Prentice Hall, p. 29.
5. This exercise was adapted from "Four Drawings" by Dr. Michie Rose. Used with permission of the author.

Chapter 10

1. Harville Hendrix. 1988. *Getting the Love You Want: A Guide for Couples.* New York: Henry Holt, p. 35.
2. Ponder, *The Dynamic Laws of Prosperity,* p. 22.

Chapter 11

1. Gawain, *Creative Visualization.*
2. David Richo, *The Five Things We Cannot Change,* p. 15.
3. Hans Selye. 1956. *The Stress of Life.* New York: McGraw-Hill.
4. Norman Cousins. 1989. *Headfirst: The Biology of Hope.* New York: E. P. Dutton.
5. Ponder, *The Dynamic Laws of Prosperity,* p. 33.
6. David Richo, *The Five Things We Cannot Change,* p. 15.

Conclusion

1. Copyright ©1993, by Portia Nelson. From the book *There's a Hole in my Sidewalk: The Romance of Self-Discovery.* Hillsboro, OR: Atria Books/Beyond Words Publishing. Used with permission.

Index

abandonment, fear of, 146–48
achieving, focus on, 2–3
acting, versus reacting, 66–69
actions, preceded by thoughts, 45
activities
   boomerang, 207, 208
   cosmic slap exercise, 112–14
   good-bye exercise, 171–73
   letting-go exercise, 133–35
   looking glass, 207
adversity, good coming out of, 89–90
Alcoholics Anonymous, 128
amygdala, 50–52
anger
   as ego part, 81
   physical results of, 202–3
approval, desire for, 17–18, 165
Art of Happiness, The (Dalai Lama and
   Cutler), 11, 94–95
Aurelius, Marcus, 27
Autobiography in Five Short Chapters, An
   (Nelson), 210–11

Beck, Aaron, 212
Beck Institute for Cognitive Therapy and
   Research, 212
Belzer, Richard, 107
blessings, coming in disguise, 70–71
boomerang activity, 207, 208
brain, ability of, to change neural
   connections, 11
Buddhism, principle of the beginner's mind,
   143
Buddhist Information and Education
   Network, 212
Buddhist monks, responding to protest, 61–62
Burns, David, 80
busyness, 149

calm, 19
Capra, Fritjof, 12–13
catharsis letter, 175
Center for Self-Leadership, 213
challenges
   refusal to accept, 125–26
   responding to, 107–11, 115–18

change
   avoiding, 64
   inevitability of, 125
   practicing, 64–65
   resistance to, 9
chicken-and-egg relationships, 204–6
Chodron, Pema, 21, 27, 108
choice, 66
   determining happiness and peace of
     mind, 88
   related to confidence, 71–74
clarity, 19, 26
clinging, 122
   meditation for, 135
closed energy, 182
collective unconscious, 198
compassion, 19, 92
complaints, seeing in context, 99
compliments
   accepting, 87–88
   turning into dispersions, 85–86
compulsive thinking, 24–25
conditioned mind, 21
confidence, xiv
   activities blocking, 123
   boomerang cycle and, 203–4
   choice related to, 71–74
   coming from inner interpretation of
     reality, 46
   dependent on state of mind, 5
   effect of, on life, 106–7
   feelings related to, 34
   formation of, 41–42
   introducing confident thoughts, 208
   learning to live with, 8
   related to awareness, 70
   sabotaging, 5–6
   self, 19
   using, to approach uncertainty, 65
   using external means to try to build, 2–3
Confidence Report Card, 14–15
Confident Life
   charting, 37–38
   creating, 8–9
   curiosity as gateway to, 28
   physical and spiritual benefits of, 11–12

❧ About the Author ❧

Bryan E. Robinson, Ph.D., is Professor Emeritus at the University of North Carolina at Charlotte and a psychotherapist in private practice. He is the author of over twenty-five books on self-awareness and relationships, including the best-selling *Heal Your Self-Esteem* (HCI) and *Chained to the Desk: A Guidebook for Workaholics, Their Partners and Children, and the Clinicians Who Treat Them* (NYU Press). His books have been translated into nine languages, and his work has been featured in major national magazines. He hosted the PBS documentary *Overdoing It: When Work Rules Your Life* and has appeared on *20/20, Good Morning America, ABC's World News Tonight, NBC Nightly News, The Early Show, CNBC's The Big Idea,* and hundreds of radio broadcasts. He resides with his partner of thirty-eight years in Asheville, North Carolina, where he maintains a clinical practice. Visit his website at www.bryanrobinsononline.com, or e-mail him at bryanrobinson@bryanrobinson.com.